Storrs Lectures on Jurisprudence
Yale Law School, 1974

The Ages of American Law

Second Edition

Grant Gilmore

With a New Foreword and
Final Chapter by Philip Bobbitt

Yale UNIVERSITY PRESS

New Haven and London

Yale University Press books may be purchased in quantity for educational,
business, or promotional use. For information, please e-mail sales.press@yale.edu
(U.S. office) or sales@yaleup.co.uk (U.K. office).

Printed in the United States of America.

Library of Congress Control Number: 2014941002
ISBN 978-0-300-18991-9 (pbk.)

10 9 8 7 6 5 4 3 2 1

Contents

Foreword

Philip Bobbitt

In late 2011, I was approached by an editor at Yale University Press, who was considering a revised edition of Grant Gilmore's classic, *The Ages of American Law*. I responded that I would be pleased if the Press would publish, as a Foreword to such an edition, my 1975 essay in the *Yale Law Journal* introducing one of Gilmore's lectures, "The Age of Anxiety," which he reworked to form Chapter 4 of the book. After reading that essay, the editor proposed that it be published as a "historical document with a preface to provide context" and that I should also draft a new section of the main text bringing it up to date, as apparently some readers wished in the classes in which the book is taught.

It is bracing to realize that something one once wrote can be referred to as a "historical document," but I must concede that I am now at the same age Gilmore was when he delivered the lectures. Nevertheless I demurred, daunted by the prospect of adding a syllable to the main text of Gilmore's masterpiece. When James Thurber was sounded out by a publisher as to whether he would be interested in doing the illustrations for a new edition of *Alice's Adventures in Wonderland,* he was outraged. "Keep the Sir John Tenniel drawings, I'll redo the text," he replied. That is rather the way I felt about tampering with Gilmore.

Yet I remained perplexed and indulged my perplexity the way I usually do, by procrastination. I had no desire to revise any of Gilmore's formulations, and I therefore wrote the editor that it would be a mistake to add to the "existing text of the book, which is so elegantly and insightfully written that it is certain to shame anything appended to it." Adding a final chapter by me would, I told her, be like "putting a garage on the side of a William Delano townhouse."

At the same time, I very much wanted the book to stay in print, and I was aware that a survey of academics who used it in their courses had revealed some considerable sentiment for an updating and had disclosed some disquiet among first-year students—a notoriously paranoid bunch—that they were being given outmoded materials to study.[1] Perhaps to accommodate that concern, I should accept the proposal and do what I could, owing to my affection for Gilmore and my history with the origins of the book. That history will take a little explaining.

During the academic year 1974–75, Gilmore and another professor at the Yale Law School, Robert Cover, supervised a writing course in which I was the only student. Cover had just published his remarkable *Justice Accused,* which, accepting Karl Llewellyn's historical and jurisprudential genealogy of Grand and Formal Styles, attempted to account for the deplorable transition from the one to the other that Llewellyn had described in his magisterial *The Common Law Tradition: Deciding Appeals.* Cover dated this transition a generation earlier than Llewellyn, locating its origin in a particular class of antebellum cases involving slavery: "[I]n slavery, the 1840s and 1850s were not a golden age of free-wheeling policy jurisprudence [in the Grand Style] but an age of the retreat to formalism."[2] American judicial opinions—including those of the most esteemed Grand Style judges like Lemuel Shaw, John McLean, and even Joseph Story—had begun to show evidence of an elemental decay into formalism as a way, Cover argued, of dealing with the conflict between the consciences of judges who deplored slavery and the manifest commands of Congress and the Constitution. Each of these great jurists was committed to abolition yet nevertheless felt compelled to render decisions upholding the institution of slavery. "Antislavery judges," Cover wrote, "consistently gravitated to the formulations most conducive to a denial of personal responsibility and most persuasive as to the importance of the formalism of the institutional structure for which they had opted."[3]

Gilmore was intrigued with Cover's thesis and planned, I learned, to structure his Storrs Lectures later that year around the Llewellyn typology. It was my aim, in the blithe way of students whose ignorance gives an unwarranted but indispensable confidence to their precocity, to show Cover and Gilmore that Llewellyn's essential premise—that American jurisprudence of Grand and Formal Styles reflected a sharp break in judicial argument—while an interesting heuristic, was an elusive if not arbitrary distinction. Why these two masters were prepared to indulge me in this fantastic conceit remains a mystery, but indulge me they did, and at the end of the year I produced a 300-page essay that they mercifully accepted—and honored—doubtless with the requirement that I graduate immediately.

Once a week, most weeks, Gilmore and I met at Mory's for lunch. In the beginning, and for some months, we acted out the familiar struggle of tutor and advisee in which the tutor tries to confine the proposals of the advisee to some manageable topic and the advisee attempts to evade any reasonable constraints in order to take up a subject as vast as he can negotiate. Gilmore wanted me to test my theory by examining the judicial constructions of the Carriage of Goods by Sea Act over a one-year period in the 1880s. I wanted to examine every recorded opinion in which a state or federal court had explicitly refused to follow Supreme Court precedent. Cover must have anticipated how obstreperous I was going to be, as I mainly remember my discussions with Gilmore over the choice of my subject.[4]

At the time, I was an article editor for the *Yale Law Journal.* When I learned that Gilmore was going to deliver the Storrs Lectures during that year, I began a campaign to persuade the *Journal* board, and Gilmore himself, that we should publish one of the lectures in the *Journal.* The Storrs Lectures are, I surmise, the most prestigious series of such addresses in American law. Lon Fuller used one such series to deliver *The Morality of Law;* others have been given by Roscoe Pound, Robert Hutchins, Bruce Ackerman, and most notably, Benjamin Cardozo, whose *The Nature of the Judicial Process* was auditioned in New Haven with much trepidation by its author who feared that his confession that in some rare cases a judge did not simply locate the applicable law and mechanically apply it would so shock the country that it would foreclose his elevation to the U.S. Supreme Court. (It didn't.)

Gilmore came at the end of a period of importance and prestige for law professors that I do not think is likely to be repeated. Even then, however, he was a very significant figure among the elect. The breadth of his work—in addition to being the most important academic of his generation in commercial law, he also coauthored, with his close friend Charles L. Black, Jr., the leading treatise on admiralty law—is unusual. Furthermore, the depth of his work—he was awarded the Ames Prize by the Harvard law faculty for his two-volume treatise on security interests in personal property, the single "most distinguished work" of the period, in addition to his being the principal draftsman of Article 9 of the Uniform Commercial Code—would have been remarkable in any era.

He stood in apostolic succession, jurisprudentially, to Arthur Corbin and Karl Llewellyn, the commercial law giants of two earlier generations, but neither of them could have written *The Ages of American Law* because Gilmore came at the end of the era of Legal Realism, an era that they had begun. *The Ages of American Law* is not really a book of legal history, a field as to which Gilmore was a committed skeptic, and I am glad to see that its use has not been confined to such courses. Rather it is a meditation on the evolution of law in the United States, a society that began as the bumptious child of English common law and eventually developed the most advanced methods of legal pragmatism, methods that are only now beginning to be adopted in the United Kingdom and around the world. As such, *The Ages of American Law* is the finest introduction to U.S. legal methods of which I am aware, written by an important figure in shaping those methods, at a time in his life when he could reflect on the course and shape of their development. It is far more accessible and engaging than Llewellyn's *The Bramble Bush,* another classic that is its only real competitor.

Yet at the *Yale Law Journal,* I faced a skeptical editorial board. Why publish only one of the lectures; what sense would it make, if severed from the argument of the full set of three? And why publish all three if they were going to be published in their entirety by Yale University Press? The solution my long-suffering editor-in-chief proposed was that we publish the final lecture, which presented the culmination of Gilmore's argument, and some sort of introduction summarizing the foregoing two lectures, which I was to write.

Here, then, is that *Law Journal* introduction,[5] followed by the most enjoyable 99 pages I know on the subject of American jurisprudence, to which has been appended a new chapter written by a devoted admirer.[6]

Editor's Introduction

On three October afternoons last fall, we attended a presentation of the Storrs Lectures, entitled "The Ages of American Law." The William Lucius Storrs Lectureship was endowed in 1889 by Mary and Eliza Robinson, in memory of their great-uncle, the Chief Justice of the Connecticut Supreme Court. The first lecture was given the following year by Judge Cooley on the Interstate Commerce Commission; he had just been appointed its first Chairman. The Storrs Lectures have remained the Law School's most distinguished lecture series; even a partial list includes some of the most influential legal figures and ideas of the past 85 years. Sometimes annually, sometimes not, a speaker from outside the Law School is invited. This year the Lectures coincided with the Sesquicentennial of the Law School, and Grant Gilmore had promised to deliver them.

Professor Gilmore is one of the most respected and best liked of a popular and respected faculty. At least part of his charm for students is his manifest disregard for anything as vulgar as popularity, for, so far as we know, he has never said a personal word, of any kind, to any student; indeed very different kinds of students claim him as their own, speculating on opinions never glimpsed beneath a deeply mannered ambivalence.

About 5'10", with a ruddy complexion and two pairs of frequently exchanged, thick-lensed glasses, Professor Gilmore has a somewhat stout, Tenniel-drawn physique. As he talks he emphasizes words through sudden and arresting changes in the clipped rumble and volume of his voice, gesturing like Theodore Roosevelt in the old reels, appearing to speak through clenched teeth beneath a bristling mustache. As he raps an open book with his glasses or chops the air in

casual impatience, his gestures remind us of someone thinking alone, trying to recall a familiar address or telephone
number. Former lecturer in French at Yale College, Reporter
for Article 9 of the UCC, coauthor of the standard treatise
in Admiralty, Ames Prize and Coif Award winner, Gilmore
seems to us, more than the Great Man, the Solitary. We anx-
iously awaited the lectures, entitled "The Age of Discovery,"
"The Age of Faith," "The Age of Anxiety."

On the afternoon of the 29th we arrived early and took
seats near the front of the long room. The room quickly filled
and the Dean introduced Professor Gilmore with a touch-
ing, if hurried pride. Gilmore seemed distracted; he wore an
uncomfortably new white shirt with corners still stiff at the
back of the collar.

He began:

> We are asked to believe that this year marks the hun-
> dred and fiftieth anniversary of the founding of this
> Law School. If that is true, the history of the School very
> nearly spans the history of American law. It seems ap-
> propriate, therefore, to devote these lectures to a review
> of the century and a half during which the Yale Law
> School and the American legal system have, at times
> somewhat uneasily, co-existed.

We sat next to Professor Deutsch and his wife, who had
been Gilmore's research assistant for the preparation of his
treatise, *Security Interests in Personal Property.* We noted
other faculty in the room who must have been students of
Gilmore's, just as he had been part of a generation trained by
Corbin.

> Before the 18th century, lawyers looked upon them-
> selves—as they were looked upon by others—as being

essentially plumbers or repairmen. By the end of the 18th century we had come to think of ourselves as phi-losophers—an upgrading of our status which the legal mind naturally found irresistible.

Gilmore then introduced the "Age of Discovery" by pre-senting its antecedents: prior to the second half of the 18th century there was no notion of a generalized theory of law. Blackstone had no predecessors. It was that half century—when "many remarkable minds set out, almost at the same time, to discover the laws of history, the laws of social and economic behavior, the laws, we might say, of law"—that encompassed America's construction of its own legal sys-tem. Having cut our political ties to England, conscious of our immense potential for wealth and power, self-critically committed to a legal system that made some kind of overall sense, we were a society poised for takeoff—a society capable of producing the Constitution.

That society confronted the task of selectively transplant-ing the English common law in a period of dizzying change (and overseas *that* law was experiencing similar stresses, evoking the creative, Mansfieldian approach to judging). To this task of constructing a ship while under sail were added the tensions of a potentially fragmenting federalism. The history of pre–Civil War American law is, in the main, an account of how law coped successfully, astonishingly—through the codification movement, through inspired judi-cial interpretation, through Kent's *Commentaries* and Story's original and impressive treatises—with the structural forces of instability.

Summing up this period, Gilmore followed Llewellyn in finding its only counterpart in the great classical period of Roman Law, the third century A.D. He ended the first lecture by saying, "The best definition of a golden age is, no doubt, that it is one which can never be repeated—or recaptured."

There was enthusiastic applause.

The following afternoon we returned to the lecture room. Well before the lecture was to begin, it became apparent that, with even the aisles already full, the lecture site would have to be moved. We decamped to the auditorium.

In a speech in 1963, Professor Gilmore had said,

> No lawyer worthy of the name can ever be either truly a conservative or truly a radical: at one and the same time we must somehow devote ourselves to the preservation of tradition, which we do not greatly respect, and to the promotion of change, in which we do not greatly believe.

Appropriately modest words for our chastened present; but for 1963? Yet we suspect that his oft-quoted epigram was not racy prescience. Rather it is a kind of gentleman's code, a statement of the perspective that structures the professional monologue of the Solitary, fastidious, ironic, aristocratic. If so, it is hardly paradoxical that the Storrs Lectures should adopt historical themes; the past, in the hands of the quick-witted, is just as unpredictable but not nearly so repetitious as the present.

Professor Gilmore spoke, that day, about "The Age of Faith." Discussing the period, roughly from the Civil War to World War I, of the "law's black night," he remarked that, paradoxically, American law had apparently achieved some of its greatest triumphs during that time. The major categories we use to study our legal system were reduced to order and certainty, indeed were invented, in this period.

Christopher Columbus Langdell, who in 1870 became the first Dean of the Harvard Law School, was the symbol of the age, and his one guiding idea the organizing principle of its energies. The idea was that law was "a science," and from this thesis several corollaries flowed. If legal truth is a species of scientific truth, then once discovered, it must necessarily endure. It follows as a methodological consequence that legal study will be devoted to the progressive simplification of formulae, and to an effort to reduce their number while increasing their explanatory power. The Langdellians thus sought, with considerable success, to design unifying theories which would embrace broad areas of the common law—theories which meant that the status of parties and the origin of their disputes were not to be taken into account.

Since hitherto the principal characteristic of American law had been its "chaotic diversity, its sensitivity to changing conditions, its fluidity," the American case law would support Langdell's theories only if it was ignored. The Langdellians did precisely that, citing a few English reports and a limited number of "right" cases in this country. At about the same time the West Publishing Company established the National Reporter System and the Langdellian revolution was complete: a precedent-based, largely nonstatutory system must have difficulty coping with such fecundity. The treatises of the period soon changed from simply identifying for the practitioner what the cases were, to stating the "correct rule," often in black letter text, and then justifying it in terms of broad generality. The supporting cases came in at the bottom of the page in typically factless string citations. Of the moving spirit of all this, Gilmore said, "Langdell seems to have been an essentially stupid man who, early in his life, hit on one great idea to which, thereafter, he clung with all the tenacity of genius."

We were sitting next to Professor Bittker and just before such lines were finished he would chuckle, always a bit more quickly, a little sooner than the rest. This both distracted and alarmed the young lady sitting next to us, who seemed unsure whether the Professor was awfully clever or had sneaked a look at the text. Of the speaker himself, we could notice a buoyant change since the first lecture. Professor Gilmore's extreme personal reticence seemed tempered by his appreciation of the institutional significance of the Lectures, and of the fact that he owned both a dramatic reading style and the face of a slightly cross-eyed Robert Benchley.

At any event, he turned next to the man whose biography he is presently writing.

"If Langdell gave the new jurisprudence its methodology, Holmes, more than anyone else, gave it its content." Holmes argued that the function of law is to channel private aggression in an orderly fashion. He wrote: "The first requirement of a sound body of law is that it should correspond with the actual feelings and demands of the community, whether right or wrong." In his radical and despairing pessimism, Holmes cut against the grain of most 19th century thought, which was characterized by an optimistic belief in the progressive amelioration of the human condition. Furthermore, he seems to have had a far more sophisticated idea about the nature of scientific inquiry than most 19th century social scientists, including the Langdellians. And, finally, he believed in the necessary instability and inconsistency of any given state of the law.

Despite all this, the lectures in which Holmes displayed these ideas to the world were enthusiastically received. Published the following year under the title *The Common Law,* they purported to be an historical survey of the development of a very few common law principles which had recurrently manifested themselves in the various subjects Holmes chose to deal with, principally tort and contract. The Langdellians, the believers in the one true rule of law, ignored Holmes's insights into the complex interplay between new materials drawn from life and old materials not quite absorbed from history, but accepted Holmes's extremely general and equally parsimonious principles of liability.

Holmes's accomplishment was to make Langdellianism intellectually respectable. In the academic world, the success was complete. Concurrently, events of the period seemed to evoke opinions from the judiciary that unconsciously embodied Langdell's notions.

The post–Civil War judicial product starts from the assumption that law is a closed logical system. Judges do not make law; they merely declare the law, which, in some Platonic sense, already exists. Seldom did judges make any attempt to explain the reasons for their own decisions; it was enough to say, "The rule which we apply has long been settled," citing numerous cases, without facts.

Langdell had nothing to do with shaping the new judicial approach. By his time we had put behind us the urgent problems which had concerned Kent and Story and had largely spent our energies in the Civil War. Even the pace of technological change seems to have slowed. Langdell was the first to sense the altered mood and give it theoretical expression. Such expression equally suited the economic movers and shakers of the day.

Referring, we hoped, to the economic theories of the early 20th century, Professor Gilmore reminded us:

> There has always been a symbiotic relationship between the academic establishment, which provides the theories, and the economic establishment, which appreciates being told that the relentless pursuit of private gain is, in the last analysis, the best way of serving the

public interest. But even the economists must have felt
a grudging admiration for the lawyers who could see
that the case of a working man bargaining with his corporate employer over wages and the case of a Vermont
farmer dickering with a summer resident over the price
of a cord of firewood could both be reduced to the paradigm of A who voluntarily contracts with B.

As Gilmore had written in another context, "Never, I dare
say, has any field of law appeared to be as perfectly structured, as free from any kind of fault or flaw, as the law of
contracts in Williston's great treatise."

Ending the second lecture, Gilmore responded to the ova-
tion with a short bow.

The third lecture, on the last day in October, was again delivered in the auditorium. Gilmore's review of our legal past
inexorably advanced on the present. The first two lectures
had prepared us for an erudite review of America's grand
designs and hopeful revolutions. Few expected what seemed
to us the savage nihilism of the third lecture, which is here
reprinted.

Twenty-five years ago, Professor Gilmore wrote of Karl
Llewellyn in these pages that he "and his co-conspirators
were right in everything they said about the law. They skill-
fully led us into the swamp. Their mistake was in being sure
that they knew the way out of the swamp: they did not, at
least we are still there." And, Gilmore suggested that afternoon, so it would inevitably be.

As we sat in the auditorium that afternoon, we had the
feeling that ironies far beyond our comprehension, beyond
even our guessing, continually pressed on Professor Gilmore.
Sometime ago, speaking of the law itself, he had written,
"The more things change, the French proverb reminds us,

the more they are the same: our gains, it may be, are illusory, but so are our losses."

The Dean introduced him once again, an introduction acknowledged this time with a confident bow. Gilmore began in his customary rumble, his thick-lensed glasses reflecting the auditorium lights. His hands chopped the air with an offhanded impatience as he dashed hopes across our eager faces. When the third lecture was over, we rose and clapped and cheered.

P.C.B.

Preface

In 1972 the dean and faculty of the Yale Law School invited me to deliver a series of lectures on the Storrs Foundation. The lectures were scheduled for October 1974 on the occasion of a convocation which marked the hundred and fiftieth anniversary of the Law School's founding. The timing suggested to me as an appropriate subject a review of American law during the century and a half of at times uneasy coexistence of the Yale Law School and the American legal system.

This book is an expanded version of the 1974 Storrs Lectures.[1] It is not—any more than the original lectures were—a contribution to the scholarly literature. I have put forward a number of hypotheses about what seems to have happened in American law since 1800 or thereabouts along with some speculations about why what seems to have happened should have happened. My hypotheses and speculations make a certain amount of sense to me. I shall be pleased if they make any sense to others. I have, however, made no attempt to "prove" the soundness of my views by the piling up of conventional documentation. The notes will serve to guide the curious reader to other discussions of some of the issues here passed in review.

My own area of expertise lies in what is usually referred to as commercial law (which, as lawyers use the term, includes the general law of contracts). The illustrations and analogies which come most readily to my mind are drawn from the material I am familiar with. If I had been an expert in

criminal law or constitutional law, the illustrations and analogies would have been drawn from those fields. The book
would, in that case, have had a different flavor; I doubt that
the argument would have been substantially different from
the one that is here presented.

Grant Gilmore
Yale Law School

Acknowledgments

I am most grateful to former Dean Abraham Goldstein and the faculty of the Yale Law School for the invitation to give the lectures on which this book is based. Dean Goldstein sat patiently through all three of the lectures—a courtesy which, I thought, was well above and beyond the scope of his duty.

I am indebted to many of my students at the Yale Law School for thoughtful suggestions and helpful criticisms in seminar papers and discussions over the past few years. In particular I should like to thank David Roe, who read over the original text of the lectures and made a great many useful comments; Philip Bobbitt, who contributed both an introduction to and editorial supervision of the lecture which was published in the *Yale Law Journal* as "The Age of Anxiety" (84 *Yale L.J.* 1022 (1975)); James D. Miller, who first drew my attention to the parallelism between the ideas of Holmes and Peirce in a paper which was published as "Holmes, Peirce, and Legal Pragmatism" (84 *Yale L.J.* 1123 (1975)); Charles Yablon, for a paper, which so far as I know has not been published, on the philosophical bases of Holmes's book, *The Common Law*.

Andrew Kossover, of the Vermont Law School, provided valuable assistance in research and showed great ingenuity and resourcefulness in running down out-of-the-way sources and references.

I also owe a debt of appreciation to Eileen Quinn and the secretarial staff of the Yale Law School, to Bea Ericson and the secretarial staff of the Vermont Law School, and to Virginia Church of Enfield, New Hampshire, who typed the final draft.

1

Introduction

I

Ever since the remote day when human beings began to live together in society, official organs of the state have been charged with the responsbility of deciding disputes between individuals who belong to the community (or are at all events temporarily within it) as well as disputes between individuals and the state. From the beginning of social time there have been institutions like courts which have generated or excreted law or something like law. In all societies beyond the most primitive a professional class of lawyers and judges has emerged and maintained itself. In most societies at most periods the legal profession has been heartily disliked by all non-lawyers: a recurrent dream of social reformers has been that the law should be (and can be) simplified and purified in such a way that the class of lawyers can be done away with. The dream has never withstood the cold light of waking reality.

Thus there has always been law and there have always been lawyers. If we are invited to think about the growth of the law within any society over a period of time, we assume, instinctively, that the growth must have been gradual, progressive, and, in some sense of the word, rational. Our instinctive assumption is wrong with respect to most societies throughout most of recorded history. If we think only of the common law of England and its adaptation in the North American colonies which became the United States, the assumption will still be wrong unless we take as our starting point the eighteenth century (in England) and the establishment of the federal republic in this country.

We know much less about the history of the common law than, for a long time, we thought we did. We are only beginning to learn something about the confused and chaotic process which led to its eventual emergence. An English scholar has admirably summed up this extraordinary development:

> How can a system of law, a system of ideas whose hypothesis it is that rules are constant, adapt itself to a changing world? It has not been the ordered development of the jurist or the legislator, of men thinking about law for its own sake. It has been the rough free enterprise in argument of practitioners thinking about nothing beyond the immediate interest of each client; and the strength of the system has been in the doggedness, always insensitive and often unscrupulous, with which ideas have been used as weapons. . . . The life of the common law has been in the unceasing abuse of its elementary ideas.[1]

The mindless, unconscious process which Professor Milsom graphically describes did, in the end, lead to the flowering of a distinctively English law—distinctive not so much for its substance as for its technique and style of adjudication. We do not know why this should have happened. Many societies have endured as long, or longer, without having produced anything comparable. But in England the royal courts, which had reluctantly assumed the jurisdiction abandoned by the local and ecclesiastical courts, had, by the sixteenth century, begun to produce the raw materials from which, in time, a coherent body of law could be put together.

From the seventeenth century on, abridgments, digests, and collections of cases began to appear in England—efforts to bring some sort of order to the accumulating chaos of the case law. These were modest or low-level intellectual enterprises. Lawyers continued to think of themselves, as they were thought of by others, as being plumbers or repairmen. The law books were essentially plumbers' manuals.

II

The idea that there should or could be such a thing as a generalized theory of the common law dates from the second half of the eighteenth century. Blackstone had no predecessors. By the end of the century, lawyers had put aside their plumbers' image and become philosophers—an upgrading of status which the legal mind naturally found irresistible. Indeed, we became students not merely of law but, much more grandly, of jurisprudence—an old word wrenched into a new meaning.[2]

The eighteenth century invented not only law or jurisprudence but also history, economics, and sociology—that is, the whole range of what came to be called the social sciences.[3] No doubt, the availability of a sufficient number of case reports was a precondition to the establishment of law as a proper subject for theoretical study. But the invention or discovery of history, economics, and sociology did not in any sense depend on a specialized body of materials like our case reports. Evidently the hypothesis which commended itself to many eighteenth-century minds was that the ideas and techniques which had proved spectacularly successful in the investigation of physical phenomena could, with equal success, be applied to the investigation of social phenomena. Scientific inquiry, as the eighteenth century understood the concept, started from the assumption that there are, in whatever may be the subject matter of the investigation, observable regularities which can be identified, described, analyzed, and understood. Once that has been done, the future course of events can be predicted. And once we know what results follow from what causes, we are in a position to control, as well as to predict, the future. Extraordinary advances had been achieved in the natural sciences. The hypothesis that there are also observable regularities in the development of human societies must have been as obvious as it was attractive. Many remarkable minds set out, almost at the same time, to discover the laws of history, the laws of social and economic behavior, the laws, we might say, of law.

The eighteenth century, with good reason, thought well of itself. It was the Age of Enlightenment. It was also an age of enthusiasm and of a generally shared belief in the inevitability of progress—a belief which sustained itself throughout the nineteenth century and into our own. This pervasively optimistic intellectual ambience guaranteed that the laws which the prototypical social scientists might discover would be laws we could be proud of and live with happily, not laws which would bring us crashing down in a hopeless despair at the human condition.

We could not have developed any theories about law before the eighteenth century. The theories which were developed naturally bore the stamp of the age in which they were first hammered out. They purported to be scientific and, at the same time, assumed that everything was—or soon would be—for the best in the best of all possible worlds. Over the past two hundred years these attitudes have done a great deal to color, cloud, or distort thinking about law in successive generations.

Blackstone's celebration of the common law of England glorified the past: without quite knowing what we were about, he said, we have somehow achieved the perfection of reason. Let us preserve, unchanged, the estate which we have been lucky enough to inherit. Let us avoid any attempt at reform— either legislative or judicial—since the attempt to make incidental changes in an already perfect system can lead only to harm in ways which will be beyond the comprehension of even the most well-meaning and far-sighted innovators.[4]

Blackstone wrote at a time when English law was going through a period of rapid, violent change. Indeed, the Blackstonian construct may well be taken as a conservative reaction to the fundamental changes which the English judges were making in the apparently settled rules of English law. Using the tools of eighteenth-century analytical "philosophy," Blackstone was in effect constructing a dike which, it could be hoped, would hold back the encroaching tide. (The use of revolutionary means to achieve a conservative end is a commonplace in the intellectual history of all societies.) And the important thing about the *Commentaries* is not that an obscure lecturer at Oxford wrote them, but that, for more than a hundred years, thousands upon thousands of lawyers and influential laymen on both sides of the Atlantic read them and believed them.

The reason for the dramatic change in English law during the second half of the eighteenth century is not far to seek. We know it as the industrial revolution. Novel methods of production and distribution required that large portions of the substantive law be rewritten in each newly industrialized country—first of all in England. Almost overnight there emerged, as independent fields of law, such commercial specialties as the law of negotiable instruments (which reflected the problems of payment and credit extension generated by the vastly increased number of mercantile transactions) and the law of sales of goods (which reflected the problems of

large-scale manufacture and of distribution in markets where
sellers and buyers could no longer deal face-to-face). There
had, of course, been cases about bills of exchange and promissory notes, as there had been cases about sales of goods, before 1750. But there is all the difference in the world between
issues which arise in litigation infrequently and irregularly
(where the results are of interest only to the parties litigant)
and issues which arise recurrently and regularly (where it becomes of the greatest importance to lawyers and their clients
to have some idea of what the law is—or, which is even more
important, what it is becoming). In that sense it is only after
1750 that it becomes possible to speak of a law of negotiable
instruments and a law of sales of goods. Later entries in the
fields of law which the industrial revolution bequeathed us
were the law of insurance, the law of secured transactions
(initially chattel mortgages, pledges, and a few conditional
sales), and, of course, the law of corporations.

As anyone who has the slightest familiarity with late
eighteenth-century English case law knows, the judges were
quite consciously aware of what they were doing: they were
making law, new law, with a sort of joyous frenzy. Lord
Mansfield was, in the eyes of his contemporaries as in those
of his successors, the greatest judge of the period.[5] In one of
his celebrated cases Mansfield had occasion to deal with the
idea that, in English law, a contractual promise is not binding
on the promisor unless it is supported by something called
consideration. (At the time Mansfield decided the case, the
term *consideration* had been in use in English case law for a
couple of hundred years but had never acquired any precise
meaning.) Mansfield's method of dealing with the problem
was characteristically brutal: he abolished the consideration
doctrine (whatever the doctrine may have been), at least (according to the report of the case) "in commercial cases among

merchants", where the defendant's promise had been given in writing. One of Mansfield's colleagues, in his own opinion in the same case, after a lengthy review of the consideration doctrine, remarked: "Many of the old cases are strange and absurd: so also are some of the modern ones. . . ."[6] In Lord Mansfield's court the judges were not true Blackstonian believers.

We might say, making use of a famous eighteenth-century formulation, that in its own time the Blackstonian thesis (which represented what the conservative establishment wanted the law to be) was confronted with its Mansfieldian antithesis (which represented what the courts were actually doing with the law during a period of extraordinary change). The resultant nineteenth-century synthesis (at the moment we are talking only of later developments in England itself) came out muddy and blurred (which is perhaps in the nature of syntheses) but with the Blackstonian elements on the whole in the ascendant. Many of Mansfield's most original contributions to the developing law of trade and commerce (and in particular his attempt to abolish the consideration doctrine) had, within a generation of his death, been rejected, flatly overruled or simply forgotten.[7]

III

In the preceding sections, the implicit assumption has been that the "beginnings" of American law are to be counted from 1800 or thereabouts. That seems to pass over, with cavalier disregard, the nearly two hundred years of our colonial history.

The development of our legal institutions during those two centuries, which makes a fascinating story, is, for a variety of reasons, irrelevant to our discussion.[8]

The law of the primitive agricultural settlements which were painfully hacked from the wilderness in the seventeenth century—indeed, the law of the westering frontier until the conquest of the continent had been completed—had no more relevance to the law of our own industrialized society than the law of the Sioux or the Cheyennes. It is true that, as the colonies prospered and their populations multiplied, courts were instituted and a professional class of lawyers and judges emerged. Even so, it is pointless to speak of an "American law" before the 1800s.

Throughout most of the eighteenth century the deepening crisis in the relationship of the colonies with England meant that our dawning national will and energy were principally focused on evading the clear mandate of the positive law. The function of colonial juries was to acquit smugglers and other violators of the Trade and Navigation Acts. The strategy of the English government was to remove litigation to the jury-less forum of the vice-admiralty courts, whose judges were appointed by the Crown. It is unlikely that a struggle for national liberation ever produces a climate which is favorable to the development of a stable legal system.

In any case, there can hardly be a legal system until the decisions of the courts are regularly published and are available to bench and bar. Even in the seaboard colonies, where the practice of law had, during the eighteenth century, become professionalized, there were no published reports;[9] consequently there was nothing which could rationally be called a legal system.

With the successful issue of the Revolution and the establishment of a centralized federal government (the degree of centralization that was intended or would be achieved was, and long remained, obscure) the stage was set for a fresh start—a fresh start in the building of political institutions, in the choice of the role which government was to play in the development of our society, in the provision of a system of law for the federal republic and its constituent states. It is entirely clear that the men who guided our affairs from the 1770s or 1780s until the 1820s or 1830s understood their unique and privileged historical situation: it does not fall to the lot of every generation to make such a fresh start in a vigorous, literate, and sophisticated society already in full flood of economic and social development, conscious of its immense potential for ever-growing power and wealth.

The fact that American law dates from the end of the eighteenth century has served to differentiate our legal system not only from that of England but from those of the Western European countries with which we share a common intellectual tradition. We never experienced the mindless process of secular growth which characterized the reemergence of legal systems in England and Western Europe after the anarchy of the Dark Ages. We sloughed off our two hundred years of colonial tutelage as if they had never been. The post-Revolutionary generation of American lawyers approached the problem of providing a new law for a new land as convinced eighteenth-century rationalists, as "philosophers" in the tradition of Voltaire, Diderot, and Montesquieu.

American law has, from its late eighteenth-century beginnings, been self-conciously and self-critically aware of itself as a system which is supposed to make some kind of overall sense. It has never been allowed to grow in the chaotic, disorganized, unplanned, eccentric confusion which, even after Blackstone, continued to mark the growth of English law. American lawyers are and always have been rationalizers, generalizers, theorists—metaphysicians, we might say, *manqués*. Our theory of precedent, for example, came to be much stricter than its English analogue. In English courts which sit in panels each judge delivers his own opinion, and the opinion of each judge who votes with the majority is as authoritative as each of the other majority opinions. Thus there are usually several versions of what an English case is supposed to mean—which frees the system up considerably. American practice early came to be that one judge writes "the opinion of the court" and his opinion contains the only authoritative statement of the case.[10] I think it is also true that the American formulation of a legal rule has always tended to be more rigid, more abstract, more universal, than the English formulation. The result has been that, particularly during periods when we have taken our precedents and our theories seriously, we have had much more trouble than the English have ever had in adjusting to changing conditions. It is not altogether fanciful to link these characteristics of the American approach to law to the fact that our system was, from the beginning, consciously designed as a sort of formal garden instead of being allowed to come up as it might from the compost heap of the centuries. Our English cousins have been the romantics of the law, We have been—at least we have tried to be—the classicists.

IV

In the following chapters I shall describe the course of American law from the early 1800s until the present and set out some hypotheses on why the changes which have occurred should have occurred when they did and as they did. It is hardly necessary to say that my own version of what happened and why it should have happened will be disputed by many respectable lawyers and historians.

I have adopted a tripartite division of our legal past which was, so far as I know, first put forward by the late Karl Llewellyn, whose last book, *The Common Law Tradition,* published in 1960, was principally devoted to what he called his "periodization" of American law.[11] Llewellyn's three "periods" run from, roughly, 1800 until the Civil War; from the Civil War until World War I; from World War I until the present (or, at all events, the recent past).

Llewellyn's book seems to be largely unread, but a great many people (either following him or having come independently to the same conclusion) have accepted the idea that there was one fundamental change—or mutation—in the American approach to law at about the time of the Civil War and another at about the time of World War I.[12] There has even developed a consensus on what the first two periods were like. The pre–Civil War period was our Golden Age. For Llewellyn this was the period of what he called the Grand Style: "style," in Llewellyn's lexicon, had nothing to do with literary felicity or its absence but referred to the process of adjudication—the way in which courts go about deciding cases. After the Civil War all the gold, by a sort of reverse alchemy, was transmuted into lead. The pre–Civil War Grand Style lost out to a Formal Style, which was as bad a way of deciding cases as the previous way had been good.

After World War I the formalistic approach which had been dominant in American legal thought for fifty years, went into a protracted period of breakdown and dissolution. There appears to be a general agreement that a principal feature of the new approach, which became manifest during the 1920s, was a root-and-branch rejection of the formalism or (in a term which came to have a wide vogue) the conceptualism of the preceding period.[13] There has been, not surprisingly, much less agreement about the positive accomplishments (if indeed there have been any) of the last fifty years.

Llewellyn had persuaded himself that, during his own professional lifetime, the pre–Civil War Grand Style had reemerged and had once again become dominant. He also seems to have thought that the pre–World War I Formal Style could be dismissed as a temporary aberration which would not (or at least need not) return. In that optimistic assessment he has had no followers. One approach which has enjoyed a considerable vogue in recent years links nineteenth-century legal formalism with nineteenth-century laissez-faire economics and the decline of formalism with the transition to the twentieth-century welfare state. A writer's attitude toward the welfare state determines his view of whether the law has been changing for the better or for the worse. What might be called the social science approach has also had its fervent advocates: that the law will change (or has been changing) for the better to the extent that the legal profession adopts (or has adopted) the theoretical insights and investigative techniques which have been developed by the social scientists, particularly the sociologists. My own approach will become evident as the discussion proceeds.

The discussion which follows will be largely concerned with legal doctrine as elaborated in judicial decisions and in law books. For two or three generations past it has been the merest truism, in much American legal writing, that the doctrine which may be found enshrined in case report and treatise is neither important nor relevant. The decisions made by courts, particularly by appellate courts, in the relatively few cases which come into litigation and are appealed are insignificant when they are compared with the decisions made by legislatures, by administrative agencies, and by the people who control large business enterprises. Therefore, the argument runs, a study of what the courts do (or of what the law professors say the courts do) is a great waste of time. The only thing that is worth studying is how decisions are made by the decision-makers who really count, among whom courts and commentators are no longer numbered.

The decisions which most dramatically affect the life of any society are not and never have been made by courts— decisions to make war (or peace), to abolish (or establish) a regime based on the private ownership of property, to enslave (or set free) all the members of a given race, to overthrow an existing government and replace it with a radically different one. These are political decisions, wise or foolish, virtuous or wicked. They have nothing to do with the concept of law, in any of the bewildering number of diverse senses in which that three-letter word is used. The need (or the opportunity) to make fundamental changes in the organization of a society occurs only at rare intervals. Most of the time we live according to established rules which will not be drawn into question until the next period of revolutionary ferment arrives. But even during periods when no one challenges the basic rules, the society we live in continues to evolve and change—in response to technological developments, to shifts in patterns of moral or religious belief, to the growth or decline of population, and so on. The process by which a society accommodates to change without abandoning its fundamental structure is what we mean by law.

In the early part of this century it was customary to draw a sharp distinction between the judicial function and the legislative function. Courts decided cases in the light of pre-existing common law or statutory rules. Only the legislature could change the rules; when the legislature had spoken, the courts were bound to carry out the legislative command. We have come to see that such a distinction is not, and never was, tenable. Courts, as Justice Holmes reminded us more than half a century ago, do and must legislate—that is, change the rules to reflect the changing conditions of life.[14] And with the progressive codification of the substantive law in this century, a significant proportion of the legislative product has come to be merely a restatement of the pre-statutory common law rules—a reworking of the judicial product designed to achieve greater simplicity and clarity.

The importance of the role which the courts have played in determining social and economic policy has varied throughout our history. Until the Civil War the legislatures, state and federal, did very little; the judges, by default, took over the task of answering the questions which someone had to answer. After the Civil War the legislatures became more active; the first administrative agencies were set up toward the end of the nineteenth century. It was also during the post–Civil War period that the idea that courts never legislate—that the judicial function is merely to declare the law that already exists—became an article of faith, for lawyers and non-lawyers alike. By the 1930s, with the prodigious legislative and regulatory effort which marked the New Deal period, it became fashionable to say that the judges had had their day, which would not come again. Nevertheless, since the end of World War II we have witnessed an extraordinary resurgence of judicial activism. The anti-judicialists of the 1930s were evidently premature in consigning the courts to the dustbin of history.

The judicial product and the literature that is based on it have played and continue to play a significant part in the evolution of our society, not only during activist periods like the present but during passive periods like the one that followed the Civil War. Furthermore, the body of doctrinal material which we shall deal with has the great virtue of being available, usable, and manageable. We may concede the obvious point that legislatures, administrative agencies, and large corporations make important decisions which affect us all and which have a great deal to do with the development of our law. It does not, however, follow that much light can be shed on, say, the process of corporate decision-making by interrogating the responsible executives. They are not trained to think that way; most of the time they will have no idea how or why they arrived at a decision; if they do know, they will not necessarily be inclined to make full disclosure to an officious intermeddler. Judges are trained to explain the reasons for their decisions. They may not always be successful, but the opinions of our better judges set a model for rational and humane discourse which the rest of us can only envy.

All generalizations are oversimplifications. It is not true that, during a given fifty-year period, all the lawyers and all the judges are lighthearted innovators, joyful anarchists, and adepts of Llewellyn's Grand Style—only to be converted en masse during the next fifty-year period to formalism or conceptualism. There are formalists during innovative periods and innovators during formalistic periods—just as there are frustrated classicists during romantic periods and frustrated romantics during classical periods. When we reconstruct the past, we think we see that in one period the innovative impulse was dominant and that in another period the formalistic impulse was dominant. We are talking about temporary swings in a continuing struggle of evenly matched forces.

Within the legal profession most practicing lawyers (who are interested in winning cases or in advising their clients in such a way that they don't have cases) prefer a formalistic approach to law. That approach holds out the promise of stability, certainty, and predictability—qualities which practitioners value highly. Judges, on the other hand, are paid to decide cases. Apart from such practices as bribery and corruption (which at times become institutionalized), judges want to decide the cases which come before them sensibly, wisely, even justly. Sense, wisdom, and justice are community values, which change as the community changes. It is a reasonable assumption that swings toward or away from legal formalism are determined by changes in community values and that such swings will be more marked in the case of the judiciary than in the case of the practicing bar.

For the past hundred years academic lawyers have constituted a third distinct segment of the profession. Professors who regularly engage in practice have disappeared from the faculties of our major law schools. (Consultation work at high fees plays the same role in academia that bribery and corruption play in the courts and, like bribery and corruption, occasionally becomes institutionalized.) Most law professors spend most of their time teaching; a few of them also write books and law review articles, whose production has for a long time been an almost exclusively academic monopoly. The academic lawyers who choose to write as well as teach lack the salutary discipline which is imposed on judges who must decide (or at least appear to decide) their cases in the light of the evidence properly introduced before them in adversary proceedings. The author of a leading article in a law review need not fear being reversed on appeal: there is no higher court. The academic legal literature which has been produced over the past hundred years shows, even more dramatically than the judicial opinions of the same period, the periodic swings toward and away from formalism. It is, however, also true that a considerable number of quirky eccentrics end up teaching law and writing law books. These are people who instinctively deny what everyone else affirms. Thus, at any given time, the literature contains a considerable amount of writing which cuts against the prevailing grain. Nevertheless, the academic literature, viewed historically, brings us as close as we are apt to come to what Justice Holmes once referred to as "the felt necessities of the time."[15]

2

The Age of Discovery

I

English law was the only law that post-Revolutionary American lawyers knew anything about. A few had studied law in England. Most had received whatever training they had in this country—by serving as apprentices in law offices or by studying at the law schools which began to spring up toward the end of the eighteenth century. But the only available sources were English sources—from the crabbed and incomprehensible pages of Coke on Littleton to the elegant superficialities of Blackstone. Collections of English cases enjoyed a wide sale—either imported from London or republished here with (as time went on) "American annotations" added. There were no treatises on American law; there were no published collections of American case reports.[1]

However conscious American lawyers may have been of the need to make a fresh start, a system of law cannot be improvised overnight. It has to come from somewhere. Conceivably the European civil law systems, more or less vaguely derived from Roman law, could have been looked to for guidance, but few American lawyers had any familiarity with the civilian literature, available for the most part only in such outlandish languages as French, German, and Latin. (If the Napoleonic codification of French law had come a generation earlier than it did, or our own Revolution a generation later, American law might well have borrowed liberally from the French codes—but, except in Louisiana, the timing was wrong.)[2]

American law had to be based on English law—in some sense and to some degree. The questions which had to be initially decided were; In what sense? and To what degree? Was the common law to be taken over lock, stock, and barrel, subject to subsequent change at the hands of American courts? Or was the common law, along with a few statutes, to be imported selectively—with the English rules entitled to recognition as American rules only when adopted in American cases by American courts? And were pre-Revolutionary English cases, and for that matter post-Revolutionary English cases, still authoritative in American courts? Or, if not authoritative, at least persuasive?

Such questions never received neat and tidy answers. They could have been answered at the time the federal Constitution was drawn up but were not. It has been argued that the intent of the framers of the Constitution was to commit to the federal Congress and the federal judiciary the responsibility for determining most substantive law questions.[3] A part was to be reserved to state courts (and legislatures) only with respect to essentially local questions—such as title to real property. Under that approach the answers to the questions of in what sense and to what degree English law (past and present) was to be brought over would shortly have been provided by the Supreme Court of the United States. However, the intent of the framers (if that had been their intent) was never carried out and, within a generation of the constitutional debates, was lost from memory. The accepted dogma came to be that the federal government was (and had been intended to be) a government of limited powers (with all other powers reserved to the states) and that, with respect to judicial com-

petence, there was no "common law of the United States"—
only a common law as declared by the courts of the states
without review by the federal courts.[4] I shall presently have
something to say about the considerable degree to which,
despite the dogma, the common law was effectively federalized. However, the constitutional settlement which had been
agreed to by the early 1800s precluded the simplest, and arguably most rational, solution of our legal problems by an
overt federalization of almost the entire body of the law.

Thus, without constitutional guidance, the courts, state
and federal, set out as joint venturers in quest of an American law. If the judges and lawyers had been left to themselves,
they would in all probability have arrived, without delay, at a
thoroughgoing English solution. There were, however, political forces at work which delayed the process of arriving at a
consensus and influenced, in ways which it would be impossible to document, what the eventual consensus was to be.

The spirit of the frontier was hostile to the idea of a court
system staffed by professionally trained judges in which clients would be represented by professionally trained lawyers.
And at the time of the Revolution and for a generation after,
the western parts of such states as New York and Pennsylvania were still frontier areas, albeit areas which were growing
rapidly in population and political power. The people who
moved restlessly westward must have been in large part those
who were impatient with the constraints of a settled society.
The romantic idea of a simple and natural justice, stripped
of all legal artifice, is always an attractive one; during the
brief periods of frontier simplicity it no doubt seemed capable of realization. The institution of lay judges was popular
throughout the country; even in New York the members of
the state senate (whatever their legal qualifications may have
been) sat with the judges on the state's highest court of appeal

until 1846. In Western states anyone who was a citizen and over twenty-one could practice law; the Abraham Lincoln bar, so-called, survived into this century.[5]

The Revolutionary trauma had instilled in many, perhaps in most, Americans, a hatred of England and all its ways—a state of mind which the untoward events which culminated in the War of 1812 prolonged for a generation after it might otherwise have disappeared. The prevalent Anglophobia led to statutes which prohibited the use of English legal materials in court proceedings, and such statutes were not restricted to the new states beyond the mountains. A New Jersey statute, enacted in 1799 and not repealed until 1819, forbade the citation not only of any English case decided later than July 4, 1776, but also (apparently without limitation of time) of "any [English] compilation, commentary, digest, lecture, treatise, or other explanation or exposition of the common law. . . ."[6] Even in states which did not go to the New Jersey extreme, it was, we may confidently assume, the part of professional wisdom for both judges and counsel to avoid, in their opinions and arguments, anything that might look like undue deference toward the common law of England.

In time both frontier romanticism and English-baiting lost their hold on the popular imagination. The law was returned to, or recaptured by, the lawyers—a process which seems to have been completed, at least in the older states, by 1820 or thereabouts. Thus the professionalization of American law was carried out not immediately after the Revolution but twenty or thirty or forty years later. The timing proved to be important in more than one way.

By 1820 a substantial body of American legal materials had accumulated. The decisions of American courts, state and federal, were being published. Books on American law were beginning to appear as well as American republications (with added local annotations) of English books and case collections. There was an indigenous base for an American law which had not existed a generation earlier. The only professional solution which can be imagined, as of the 1780s, would have been a total borrowing of English law, which would then have been adapted, bit by bit and piece by piece, to fit the conditions of American life. In the 1820s such a total borrowing was no longer necessary. We had our own cases. Our courts were long-established institutions. American judges—Marshall and Story on the Supreme Court of the United States, Chancellor Kent in New York, and others—enjoyed a well-merited prestige. We no longer needed the totality of English law, although, with the abatement of anti-English feeling, we could profitably borrow from the inexhaustible storehouse of the English case law (including the current English cases).

Another consequence of the enforced delay in settling on the bases of our legal system was that we could look to English law, particularly the law relating to trade and commerce, as that law had been reshaped, or invented, by Lord Mansfield and his colleagues. In England itself the tide was already beginning to turn against Mansfield: his radical approach to the problem of judicial law-making was in course of being scrapped in favor of a quasi-Blackstonian approach which emphasized adherence to precedent.[7] In this country, however, a pure Mansfieldianism flourished: not only were his cases regularly cited but his lighthearted disregard for precedent, his joyous acceptance of the idea that judges are supposed to make law—the more law the better—became a notable feature of our early jurisprudence. Justice Story, in particular, both in his opinions and in his non-judicial writings, never tired of acknowledging his indebtedness to, and his reverence for, Lord Mansfield.

The fact that we did not seriously set about building an American legal system until well after 1800 also meant that the society for which the law was being provided was no longer the agricultural society which Thomas Jefferson had hoped would be our permanent state. By the 1820s the process of industrialization was far advanced. The profound shock of technological change was already being experienced, as the eighteenth-century world of stagecoaches and cottage manufacture was metamorphosed into the new and unsettling world of railroads and factories. The problems which our industrializing society faced in the 1820s were not unlike those which the English courts had dealt with fifty or seventy-five years earlier—which may have been a factor in our enthusiastic acceptance of Mansfieldianism.

Finally, the delay meant that the task of building a legal system had to be approached in the light of the constitutional settlement which had apparently denied to the federal government and the federal courts the power to insure that our emerging law would be nationally uniform, to the extent that national uniformity was, as to some degree it obviously was, essential. The danger of a state-by-state fragmentation of the substantive law became a matter of concern to many observers.[8] Some way had to be found of achieving the national uniformity which the received constitutional dogma seemed to make impossible. Indeed, the quest for uniformity has ever since remained one of our most urgent goals of law reform. With what may be the American genius for steering a middle course between extremes, the quest has never been entirely successful but the dangers of fragmentation have never been entirely realized either. The course of our legal development has been decisively influenced by the shifting fortunes of this continuing struggle. During the pre–Civil War period the proponents of national uniformity—who were never a coherently organized group—seem to have hit on several courses of action, all of which, even though they may appear to have been mutually inconsistent, were diligently pursued.

II

The first national uniformity proposal which was seriously put forward was a call for a general codification of the law.[9] In England, Jeremy Bentham had been the first advocate of codification, although he was a prophet without honor in his own country.[10] So far as we can tell, Bentham had no great influence in this country either. Bentham himself, in 1811, had proposed to President Madison the project of a comprehensive federal code, with Bentham as the draftsman. Madison, who had other matters to preoccupy him, did not take up the offer. There is no reason why Bentham should have been familiar with current developments in American constitutional law, but, even at the time when he composed his letter to Madison, a federal codification was no longer a political possibility: that debate was over and done with.

The movement in favor of codification at the state level—a proposal which was eloquently supported by Justice Story as early as 1821—was not Benthamite either in its inspiration or in its detail.[11] For Story and others, codification seemed to be the most promising way—perhaps the only way—of dealing with the problem posed by the mounting flood of case reports (already, at that early date, felt to be unmanageable) as well as with the problem of a substantive law fragmented into as many subdivisions as there were states (with the number of new states increasing decade by decade). It was assumed, and the assumption may well have been correct, that if a leading state—New York or Massachusetts, for example— codified its law, the other states would adopt the New York or

Massachusetts Code and in that way the law would become uniform throughout the country. Furthermore, in Story's peculiarly American version of the codification idea, what was needed was not a universal codification—such a project, Story once commented, would be "positively mischievous, or inefficacious, or futile"—but a limited one, restricted to fields of law which had achieved maturity, stability, and a general acceptance (he suggested "commercial contracts" as an example of what he had in mind).[12] It is true that David Dudley Field, who became the leader of the New York codification movement and who had been influenced not only by the French codes but also, quite possibly, by Bentham, had a much more ambitious vision of codification than Story ever had.[13]

Since the pre–Civil War codification movement ultimately failed—after having come within a hair's breadth of success in New York—we tend to under-estimate the influence which it exerted for the better part of half a century. The codification idea had a large popular following for reasons which had nothing to do with the sophisticated theories of professionals like Story and Field. The codifiers did not think of themselves as idealistic reformers dedicated to a lost cause. They were practical men who had caught hold of a good idea whose time had, as they and many others felt, come. From the 1820s until the Civil War, American lawyers lived with the idea that the common law not only could be but probably would be codified—that the general principles which underlay the cases, in their hundreds and their thousands, could be and probably would be set out in a connected series of reasoned propositions. That way of thinking about the law no doubt contributed to the extraordinary flexibility—the open-endedness—which became a characteristic of American law during this period.

The national uniformity idea, which had been one of the motivating forces behind the codification movement, expressed itself, in a different guise, through the early provision of a specifically American legal literature. If the law could not be unified by the enactment of uniform statutes—or codes—throughout the country, perhaps it could be unified through an authoritative formulation in learned treatises. Nothing comparable to the American treatises which soon appeared in profusion had, at that time, been seen in England. Chancellor Kent's significantly entitled *Commentaries on American Law*—originally lectures which he had given at Columbia College beginning in 1823, following his retirement from the bench—were published between 1826 and 1830 and enjoyed a fabulous (although, in my own opinion, unmerited) success: as late as 1872 they appeared in a twelfth edition, edited by a recent graduate of the Harvard Law School named Oliver Wendell Holmes, Jr.[14] Beginning in 1831 Justice Story moonlighted as Dane Professor of Law at Harvard and, by the time of his death in 1845, had produced nine major treatises and had planned to begin work on a tenth— on admiralty—the following year.[15] The Story treatises, like Kent's *Commentaries,* were quite consciously designed to lay the foundations for an American law derived from but in no sense confined by the principles of English law. The treatises, unlike the *Commentaries,* were works of impressive scholarship and of great originality. Nothing like them, in English, had ever been seen before; for the better part of a hundred years no books of comparable excellence were produced in any English-speaking country. The Story treatises remained in print as late as the 1900s; their vogue and their authority were by no means restricted to this country. Story's remarkable powers of analysis have been obscured by a style which, for twentieth-century tastes, is one of intolerable prolixity.

Any reader who can adjust himself to the stylistic conventions of the first half of the nineteenth century will find a great deal to admire, even to marvel at, in Story's thousands of pages.

There was evidently money to be made writing—or, at all events, publishing—law books. Following the great success of Kent and Story, a professional class of law-book writers emerged. For the most part these writers were not academics nor were they distinguished practitioners or judges. They were hacks who would run up a book on negotiable instruments this year, a book on corporations next year, and a book on insurance the year after that. The books were conceived as manuals for practitioners and were mostly uncritical collections of case digests. The best of them, however, were astonishingly good and, until the West Publishing Company established the National Reporter System in the 1880s, they were the essential stock-in-trade of the working lawyer.[16]

By the time of the Civil War a comprehensive legal literature, specifically directed to American doctrines and American developments, had been provided. It was a literature which, apart from such exceptional accomplishments as Story's, had no jurisprudential pretensions whatever. And yet, even the dreariest hack does, to some extent, organize his material, does impose an orderly sequence, does try to make sense of what is going on. The first flowering of our legal literature contributed greatly to the continuing struggle to keep an American law in being.

Even though the idea of a wholesale federalization of the substantive law was rejected at an early stage, the Supreme Court of the United States has, throughout our history, discovered and exploited various methods of establishing federal supremacy—and thus national uniformity.

One of these methods has been to give an expansive reading to the powers conferred by the Constitution on the federal government and the federal courts. The most dramatic example of this process during the pre–Civil War period was the Supreme Court's progressive expansion of the admiralty jurisdiction ambiguously conferred on the federal courts by Section 2 of Article III.[17] The constitutional grant covered "all causes of admiralty and maritime jurisdiction." By the time of the Civil War the Supreme Court had completed the process of construing that provision to mean that, with a few whimsical exceptions, federal law governed all aspects of the shipping industry and extended, territorially, to the inland lakes and rivers as well as to the coastal waters and the high seas. The Court's construction of the "admiralty and maritime jurisdiction" clause becomes more interesting when it is understood that the entire history of admiralty law both in England and in the North American colonies suggested (indeed, if the history was to be taken seriously, compelled) a much, much narrower reading. Thus, by the simple expedient of paying no attention whatever to the known meaning of the words chosen by the constitutional draftsmen, the Court effectively federalized—nationalized—the law relating to all waterborne transportation.

The federalizing Supreme Court also succeeded in reversing, for all practical purposes, the outcome of the constitutional debate which had allocated control of the substantive law to the states. My reference is to the celebrated case of *Swift* v. *Tyson*, decided in 1842, with Justice Story (who had been the Court's principal spokesman in the expansion of the admiralty jurisdiction) writing the opinion for a substantially unanimous Court.[18] The doctrine of *Swift* v. *Tyson* was that the federal courts would exercise an independent judgment—that is, would not be bound by the law of any state—in questions of, as Story put it, general commercial law. All lawyers know the ignominious end which, a hundred years later, was reserved for *Swift* v. *Tyson*.[19] Most of us no longer know what the case was about or what the doctrine which Story announced for the Court was or how it worked. These matters will be worth a few minutes of our time.

The case involved a technical, but by no means unimportant, point of negotiable instruments law: whether an indorsee of a bill of exchange, who had taken it in payment of a pre-existing debt, held the bill free of defenses available between the original parties. If the indorsee had paid money for the bill, he would unquestionably have held free of the defenses. Without going into the merits of the question, it suffices to say that no student of negotiable instruments law, from the time that law began to take its modern shape in the late eighteenth century down to the present time, has ever doubted that antecedent debt and new value should, for this purpose, be treated as functional equivalents.

Swift v. *Tyson* came to the Supreme Court from the federal court in New York. The defendant, Tyson, had accepted the bill in New York City. For that reason it was assumed that the case was governed by New York law (if indeed the law of any state was relevant). On the point at issue, New York law had fallen into a certain amount of confusion. Chancellor Kent, who knew his negotiable instruments law, had held in a case called *Coddington* v. *Bay*[20] that a purchaser who had taken a bill under suspicious circumstances and outside the usual course of business was not protected but added that taking a bill in payment of a debt was entirely within the usual course of business. Kent was affirmed on appeal to the Court of Errors (which was then the highest court in the state). However, careless language in the opinion in the Court of Errors apparently misled some lower court judges, with the result that there were a couple of recent (as of 1842) lower court decisions which had got the preexisting debt question wrong.

It is always a matter of great interest when a sophisticated court chooses to ignore an obvious solution to a simple case and instead elects to use the case as a vehicle for making an important doctrinal pronouncement. The obvious solution to *Swift* v. *Tyson* was to have pointed out that the only authoritative statement of New York law on the preexisting debt question had been by Chancellor Kent in *Coddington* v. *Bay* (as well as in his *Commentaries*). Careless dicta in the Court of Errors and the subsequent confusion of a few lower court judges were entitled to no weight. Thus the law of New York coincided with that of the rest of the civilized world and there was no need to go any further. Story's opinion makes it entirely clear that he understood the point. Therefore the conclusion is inescapable that he and his colleagues had decided to use this ridiculous case as the opportunity for federalizing—or nationalizing—a large part of the common law of the United States. Indeed, the arguments of counsel, which are summarized at length in the report, reinforce that conclusion. Mr. Dana, technically the losing counsel, made a brilliant argument in which, in effect, he gave aid and comfort to his nominal adversary, Mr. Fessenden. Neither Dana nor Fessenden even pretended to take the New York cases seriously. Perhaps the truth was that *Swift* v. *Tyson* was a made up case in which everyone concerned had agreed that the minor confusion in the New York law of negotiable instruments provided an admirable opportunity for inviting the Supreme Court of the United States to take a great leap forward toward the goal of a nationally uniform law.

Story's uncharacteristically brief opinion was a masterpiece of disingenuousness. He would have had the reader believe that the interesting question of whether the federal courts were bound by state rules of decisional law—technically a question of construction of the Rules of Decision Act of 1789—had never before occurred to him or his colleagues. Blandly ignoring the many available authorities which had accumulated during his own long tenure on the Court,[21] he wrapped up the argument in half a page. The answer was that federal courts should pay respectful attention to the decisions of state courts but, except for issues of essentially local interest, should decide cases in the light of general principles.[22] Indeed, Story seemed to suggest that, under the ultimate superintendence of the Supreme Court, there would be only one nationalized law in state as well as in federal courts. He closed this crucial passage with a rousing tag from Cicero to the effect that the day will come when the law will be the same in Rome and in Athens and throughout the world—*apud omnes gentes, omni tempore, una eademque lex.* He then added a magisterial review of the development of negotiable instruments law on the antecedent debt question and called it a day.

The point about *Swift* v. *Tyson* is that it was immediately and enthusiastically accepted. No one suggested that it was an unconstitutional usurpation of power by power-crazed judges or that it was a trick played by a wily Federalist justice on his unsuspecting Jacksonian colleagues. No bumper stickers called for Justice Story's impeachment. On the contrary, the doctrine of the general commercial law was warmly welcomed and expansively construed, not only by the lower federal courts but by the state courts as well.[23] For the next half century the Supreme Court of the United States became a great commercial law court. As novel issues generated controversy and conflict, the court's function was to propose a generally acceptable synthesis. The Justices, not having been divinely inspired, did not always succeed, but in a surprising number of instances they were able to produce solutions which promptly became the law of the land, whatever the forum of litigation might be.[24]

The virtues of the *Swift* v. *Tyson* idea as a device for achieving national uniformity are obvious. Less obvious, but, it may be, even more important, was the approach to the process of adjudication which Story's *Swift* v. *Tyson* opinion counseled. Courts, said Story, should not take a narrow view of precedent. They should look to the entire range of the available literature, scholarly as well as judicial, English and European as well as American. They should take into account the social and economic consequences of their decisions. Story was preaching what would be somewhat barbarously referred to a hundred years later as a policy-oriented approach to law. That approach accurately reflected the creative and innovative spirit which was a noteworthy feature of American law during the pre–Civil War period. The *Swift* v. *Tyson* opinion was one of the most eloquent, as it was one of the most influential, statements of what that spirit was.

A feature of the American approach to law which has always bewildered and not infrequently shocked foreign observers is that our courts routinely assume jurisdiction over issues which in most other countries are thought to lie well beyond the limits of judicial competence. Alexis de Tocqueville noticed this, and was impressed by it, in the 1830s:[25] thus the exercise of what was, by comparative standards, an extraordinary degree of judicial power was a phenomenon which had rooted itself in our practice well before the Civil War. The early assumption by the Supreme Court of the United States of the power to declare acts of Congress, as well as the acts of state legislatures and the decisions of state courts, unconstitutional was only the tip of the iceberg. From the beginning our courts, both state and federal, seem to have been willing to answer any conceivable question which any conceivable litigant might choose to ask. And from the beginning—which is even more curious—the American people, which throughout most of our history has distrusted lawyers, seems to have acquiesced in, indeed to have enthusiastically welcomed, the arrogation of unlimited power by the judges.

I assume that this distinctively American development was the unplanned result of the several aspects of our pre–Civil War history which we have been discussing. We did cut ourselves loose from the English tradition. We did set out to create a rationally organized system of law. We did have to adjust that system—somehow—to the dizzying pace of social, economic, and technological change. We did have to cope, in the real world, with the complicated problems which arose from the obscure metaphysical concept of an indissoluble union of indestructible states. The federal Congress did little; the state legislatures did less. The judges became our preferred problem-solvers.

The broad—indeed unlimited—range of issues which came to be committed to the courts for final solution added still another dimension to the American concept of law.

III

There was one issue—the issue which eventually tore the Union apart—which neither the judges nor any one else could control or deal with. The judicial contribution to the ongoing debate about slavery may have served to aggravate the situation and precipitate the catastrophe.[26]

Few people, in the modern world, have questioned the proposition that slavery is morally wrong. Whether slavery, at least under some circumstances, is economically right is a different question.[27] However, the economic rightness of slavery—say, in our Southern states during the nineteenth century—is irrelevant to what we feel (or what the people who lived then felt) about the institution itself. Let it be conceded that the use of slave labor was the best or the cheapest or the most efficient way of growing cotton. No amount of economic benefit could weigh in the balance against the universal moral condemnation of chattel slavery. An economic justification of slavery would stand on the same footing as Dean Swift's Modest Proposal for solving the chronic deficiency of meat in the Irish diet by having the Irish eat the large and unwanted surplus of babies.

The great and wicked compromise, without which there could never have been a federal union, was the recognition of slavery (a word which is never used in the Constitution) as an arrangement entitled to constitutional protection. In the 1780s, most people, both in free states and in slave states, may well have assumed that slavery would disappear in the South as it already had in the North. But, despite the abolition of the foreign slave trade in 1808, the institution flourished and even developed its own apologists; after the 1820s or 1830s the conditions of enslavement seem to have become progressively harsher and more inhumane. Nevertheless, the powers of the federal government (including the federal courts) had to be mobilized to protect the slaveholder's property, wherever that property might be found.

What is a judge to do when, in his judicial capacity, he is required to enforce a law which, as a private person, he regards as profoundly immoral? Many judges, in the South as well as in the North, confronted that dilemma. For Southern antislavery judges the problem was the institution of slavery itself, in all its ramifications. For Northern antislavery judges the problem came up mostly in proceedings under the Fugitive Slave Act to force the return of escaped slaves (or alleged slaves) to their owners.

A judge so situated has several options. He can resign his judgeship. Or he can offer himself as a candidate for impeachment by saying: I regard this law as immoral and refuse to enforce it in my court. Or he can evade the issue by seizing on minor technical lapses (usually procedural) and dismissing the case. Or he can enforce the law, with death in his heart—because it is the law, duly established by the constituted authorities, and because, as a judge, he has no other choice.

In the real world most judges follow either the route of technical evasion (which exalts procedural detail over substance) or the route of blind obedience (which exalts a sort of Platonic idea of the law over reality). Either route leads its followers to or toward a formalistic conception of law in which the purpose for which a rule of law exists is lost from sight; in which the law, which must always be looked on as a means, becomes its own end; in which the letter lives while the spirit dies.

Justice Story of the Supreme Court and Chief Justice Shaw of Massachusetts are among the notable judicial figures of the period who are known to have been convinced antislavery men. Much of this chapter testifies to Story's extraordinary contributions to the development of our law. Shaw was also one of our great judges—less erudite than Story, not a scholar on the bench but a man who enjoyed grappling with novel and difficult issues, which he did with tough-minded originality.[28] It fell to the lot of both men to write opinions in slavery cases.[29] In these opinions they seem to have been driven into a formalism which was entirely foreign to the ideas they had expressed and the principles they had stood for during their long careers.[30]

One of the hidden costs of the national agony which culminated in the Civil War may have been the crippling of our legal system. If judges like Story and Shaw were driven into formalism, so were many lesser judges. And once the tools of formalism have been used, even in a good cause, they are there, ready to hand, tempting. It is among other things extremely easy to decide cases according to the letter of a statute or of an established rule of law, without further inquiry. The intolerable pressures to which even Story and Shaw succumbed may have been responsible for the first appearance of the techniques of formalism in our case law. Those techniques, however, had a long and brilliant future ahead of them.[31]

IV

Karl Llewellyn once observed that what he called the Grand Style in pre–Civil War American cases was an unusual thing to find in the legal history of any society. He had found no traces of such a style in any of the other modern legal systems—principally English and German—with which he was familiar. One of the few periods in the past in which a comparable style had flourished was, he suggested, the classical period of Roman jurisprudence—roughly the third century of our era.[32] If there is anything in the Roman law analogy, we might hypothesize that by the third century it had become clear that the parochial law of the city-state which Rome had once been no longer served the needs of a world empire. Thus in Rome in the third century, as in the United States in the nineteenth century, a stable, wealthy, and powerful society found both the need and the opportunity to create a rational system of law. We know little enough about what happened in Rome during the third century and nothing at all about why, after half a century, the explosion of creative energy should have spent itself, never to be repeated, as the Roman world stumbled toward its doom.

In our history, as in the history of Rome, the period of glorious achievement came, almost overnight, to its end. No golden age endures forever—even if the barbarians do not invade, even if all the slaves are freed. In the history of literature and the arts we are familiar with the phenomenon of a great creative period which vanishes as suddenly and as unexpectedly as it came—the Elizabethan theater at the end of the sixteenth century and the Viennese school of music at the end of the eighteenth are two obvious examples among many. It may be that, for reasons which escape our grasp, the best and most creative minds of a generation are drawn to a particular field—which may be the creation of a new kind of theater or of a new style of music or, as in the North American colonies after 1750, the creation of a new kind of government or, as in our federal republic after 1800, the creation of a system of law. After a generation or two of intense activity the job is done; the best and most creative minds of the next generation follow their genius into new fields. But it will be a long time before anyone realizes that the last great play has already been written, the last great symphony composed.

3

The Age of Faith

I

My description of American law before the Civil War sounded like a romp through the Garden of Eden. Wherever we went we paused to admire the happy sight of great judges deciding great cases greatly, aware of the lessons of the past but conscious of the needs of the future, striking a sensitive balance between the conflicting claims of local automony and national uniformity in an immense, diverse, and rapidly growing country, creating a new law for a new land. Only the issue of slavery, which cast an ever-lengthening shadow, disturbed the tranquillity of the scene.

When we turn to our next period—roughly from the Civil War to World War I—we find ourselves expelled from our lovely sunlit garden and condemned to wander uncertainly in the law's black night. And yet American law apparently achieved its greatest triumphs during this period. Never had lawyers and judges and the new breed of law professors been so confident, so self-assured, so convinced beyond the shadow of a doubt, that they were serving not only righteousness but truth. Never had the idea of law as the ultimate salvation of a free society—a government not of men but of laws—so captured the imagination of any people. Never before had any society taken a professional man of law— Holmes, about whom I shall have more to say presently—as the embodiment of its dream. Perhaps, when everyone is blind, it is child's play to persuade ourselves that we now see better than our sighted predecessors ever did.

Christopher Columbus Langdell, who in 1870 became the first dean of the Harvard Law School, has long been taken as a symbol of the new age.[1] A better symbol could hardly be found; if Langdell had not existed, we would have had to invent him. Langdell seems to have been an essentially stupid man who, early in his life, hit on one great idea to which, thereafter, he clung with all the tenacity of genius. Langdell's idea evidently corresponded to the felt necessities of the time. However absurd, however mischievous, however deeply rooted in error it may have been, Langdell's idea shaped our legal thinking for fifty years.

Langdell's idea was that law is a science. He once explained how literally he took that doubtful proposition:

> [A]ll the available materials of that science [that is, law] are contained in printed books. . . . [T]he library is . . . to us all that the laboratories of the university are to the chemists and physicists, all that the museum of natural history is to the zoologists, all that the botanical garden is to the botanists. . . .[2]

From that basic proposition several subsidiary propositions followed.

Ideologically, it followed that legal truth is a species of scientific truth. The quality of scientific truth, as most nineteenth-century minds understood it, is that once such a truth has been demonstrated, it endures. It is not subject to change without notice. It does not capriciously turn into its own opposite. It is, like the mountain, there. The jurisprudential premise of Langdell and his followers was that there is such a thing as the one true rule of law which, being discovered, will endure, without change, forever. This strange idea colored, explicitly or implicitly, all the vast literature which the Langdellians produced.

The methodological consequences of "law is a science" may have been even more fateful than the ideological consequences. Scientific advance is generally thought to consist of progressive simplification. The better the hypothesis, the more phenomena it will explain. The fewer the formulas that are needed to explain whatever it is that we are investigating, the better.

Langdell put the idea this way:

> [T]he number of fundamental legal doctrines is much less than is commonly supposed; the many different guises in which the same doctrine is constantly making its appearance, and the great extent to which legal treatises are a repetition of each other, being the cause of much misapprehension. If these doctrines could be so classified and arranged that each should be found in its proper place, and nowhere else, they would cease to be formidable from their number.[3]

The Langdellians sought, with considerable success, to formulate theories which would cover broad areas of the common law and reduce an unruly diversity to a manageable unity. Let us, by way of example, consider the development of what came to be called the law of contract.

Contract liability, as we think of it, is liability imposed on a defendant who has voluntarily undertaken some obligation which, without excuse, he has failed to perform, his unexcused failure having caused loss to (or prevented gain by) the person in whose favor the obligation runs. Historians tell us that English law for several centuries after the Norman Conquest did not recognize liability for a failure or refusal to perform a promised undertaking; liability was imposed only for a faulty attempt to perform which resulted in loss or damage (typically physical).[4] Thus I could not recover damages from a blacksmith who had promised to shoe my horse but had not done so (even if it was entirely clear that the unavailability of my horse had caused me loss). However, if the blacksmith did shoe the horse but did it in such a way that the horse came up lame, I could recover damages for the injury to the horse in an action of trespass. During the sixteenth century the courts began to impose liability for breach of a purely promissory undertaking. The new action in which I could recover damages from the blacksmith for his failure to shoe the horse at all was called assumpsit; sixteenth-century lawyers seem to have looked on assumpsit as a spin-off from an action called trespass on the case (or case), which was itself a liberalized version of the original action of trespass. (Trespass and case are looked on as the ancestors of what we call tort; assumpsit is looked on as the ancestor of what we call contract.) Assumpsit in time was subdivided into special assumpsit, general assumpsit, and indebitatus assumpsit—the details of which we need not inquire into (indeed for a hundred years only a few historians have had even the vaguest idea about what the difference between, say, special assumpsit and general assumpsit could have been). No one ever developed a theory of assumpsit. In a preindustrial society, contract liability, however it might be referred to, was not a matter of much importance: Blackstone devoted only a few pages to it.

With the industrial revolution contract liability became all important—indeed the word *contract* began to displace the word *assumpsit* in the legal vocabulary, and the first books on contracts appeared in England.[5] The first American book on contracts was not published until 1844.[6] The terminological shift from *assumpsit* to *contract* suggests, no doubt, a recognition of change. Even so, in the pre-Langdellian era, no one thought of developing a theory of contract any more than any one had ever thought of developing a theory of assumpsit. There were as many types of contracts as there were classes of people to enter into them: contracts of factors, brokers, auctioneers, executors and administrators, trustees, seamen, corporations, guardian and ward, masters of ships, guarantors, landlord and tenant—and on and on in a never-ending list.[7]

In a pluralistic age, no one saw any reason why all these types of contracts should be subjected to a unitary set of rules: each class of contractors could be left to work out arrangements appropriate to the relevant trade, business, or profession. In the early books, general theoretical discussion—the consideration doctrine, the theory of conditions, the requirement of mutual assent—was minimal or nonexistent. What counted was what real people were doing in the real world.

With the Langdellians all that changed. The key to the general theory of contract which quickly emerged was that a unitary set of rules was now to cover all possible situations.[8] The status of the contracting parties and the subject matter of their deal were no longer to be taken into account. The law, under the new dispensation, no longer recognized factors or brokers, farmers or workers, merchants or manufacturers, shipowners or railroads, husbands or wives, parents or children—only faceless characters named A and B, whoever they might be and whatever it might be they were trying to accomplish.

What happened on the contract side was duplicated on the tort side. The word *tort* itself was a new invention which, for a generation or so, was used hesitantly, along with a parenthetical explanation of what the word was supposed to mean.[9]

Until the second half of the nineteenth century lawyers had not seen any need for a single word—or concept—which would cover all sorts of liability imposed for non-contractual loss, damage, or personal injury suffered by a plaintiff as the result of a defendant's wrongful acts. No one had ever thought that a unitary set of rules could (or should) be developed which would apply to trespass, case, conversion, fraud, misrepresentation, assault, and so on.[10] A general theory of torts (or wrongs) had been as foreign to the legal imagination as a general theory of assumpsit or contracts had been. But first the word and then the theory were quickly provided. As with the new theory of contracts, the new theory of torts was designed to cover all possible situations in which any A might be ordered to pay damages to any B to compensate him for personal injury or property damage, with as little account as possible being taken of who A and B were and the particular circumstances of their confrontation.

Langdell had pointed out that the law library was our laboratory and that the printed case reports were our experimental materials. It followed, therefore, that we were to study the cases and that, in our teaching, case-books were to replace treatises. It was, however, no part of Langdell's scheme that we were to study all the cases.

> [T]he cases which are useful and necessary for [the purpose of mastering legal principles or doctrines] bear an exceedingly small proportion to all that have been reported. The vast majority are useless, worse than useless, for any purpose of systematic study.[11]

Thus the vast majority of all reported cases, past and present, are worse than useless and should be disregarded. The function of the legal scholar, whether he is writing a treatise or compiling a casebook, is to winnow out from the chaff those very few cases which have ever been correctly decided and which, if we follow them, will lead us to the truth. That is to say, the doctrine—the one true rule of law—does not in any sense emerge from the study of real cases decided in the real world. The doctrine tests the cases, not the other way around.

Langdell, in his pioneering casebook on contracts, introduced the device, which long remained in fashion, of relying almost entirely on sequences of English cases, arranged chronologically; he admitted a few sequences of New York and Massachusetts cases but no other American jurisdictions were recognized. There was no other way in which the ideal of the one true rule of law could have been realized. Since 1800 the principal characteristics of American law had been its chaotic diversity, its sensitivity to changing conditions, its fluidity, its pluralism. All that had to be suppressed. I might add that no American law student or lawyer or, for that matter, judge was then, any more than now, in a position to know whether the relatively few English cases which the Langdellians admitted to the pantheon of correct doctrine were in any sense representative of what English law was or at any time in the past had been. It is also fair to say that the Langdellians, both in their casebooks and their treatises, performed major surgery on what their chosen English cases had been about when they were real cases in a real England.[12] England became our never-never land, our Shangri-La, our Utopia.

II

If Langdell gave the new jurisprudence its methodology, Holmes, more than any one else, gave it its content. However, the Langdellians—the members of the orthodox Establishment, we might say—rejected, ignored, or perhaps simply misunderstood many aspects of Holmes's complex thought. What they picked up and put to their own simpleminded use was a sort of bowdlerized, expurgated version of what Holmes had actually said.[13]

Holmes is a strange, enigmatic figure. Put out of your mind the picture of the tolerant aristocrat, the great liberal, the eloquent defender of our liberties, the Yankee from Olympus. All that was a myth, concocted principally by Harold Laski and Felix Frankfurter, about the time of World War I.[14] The real Holmes was savage, harsh, and cruel, a bitter and lifelong pessimist who saw in the course of human life nothing but a continuing struggle in which the rich and powerful impose their will on the poor and weak. Holmes had no use for the gentle optimism of Karl Marx who seems to have believed that after one more revolution the world would be a better place. According to Holmes:

> [T]he *ultima ratio*, not only *regum*, but of private persons, is force, and . . . at the bottom of all private relations, however tempered by sympathy and all the social feelings, is a justifiable self-preference. If a man is on a plank in the deep sea which will only float one, and a stranger lays hold of it, he will thrust him off if he can. When the state finds itself in a similar position, it does the same thing.[15]

In this bleak and terrifying universe, the function of law, as Holmes saw it, is simply to channel private aggressions in an orderly, perhaps in a dignified, fashion. He reduced all of jurisprudence to a single, frightening statement:

> The first requirement of a sound body of law is, that it should correspond with the actual feelings and demands of the community, whether right or wrong.[16]

That is, if the dominant majority (which seems to be what Holmes meant by "the community") desires to persecute blacks or Jews or communists or atheists, the law, if it is to be "sound," must arrange for the persecution to be carried out with, as we might say, due process. If the law does not adopt popular prejudices, whatever they may be, the only alternative, Holmes went on to explain, is private—that is, extra-legal—retribution against the despised minorities.

Holmes, in his radical and despairing pessimism, cut against the grain of most nineteenth-century thought. Holmes also differed from most of his contemporaries in his understanding of the nature of scientific inquiry. Holmes by no means rejected the "law is a science" idea, but his own ideas about the scientific method and the qualities of scientific truth were at a far remove from those accepted as self-evident by most nineteenth-century minds.

Holmes's thinking may have been influenced by his membership in a group of young men who, calling themselves the Metaphysical Club, met regularly in Boston and Cambridge from 1870 to 1872. William James was one of the members. Another was a man named Charles Peirce who, almost unknown in his own lifetime, has since his death acquired a considerable vogue among philosophers.[17] Peirce held strikingly original views both about the nature of scientific inquiry and about the nature of knowledge. Peirce did not look on scientific inquiry as a method of discovering or revealing truth. His hypothesis was that inquiry is a never-ending process whose purpose is to resolve doubts generated when experience does not mesh with preconceived theory. When the relevant community of investigators has arrived at a consensus which provides a new basis for belief, the unpleasant sensation of doubt is, for a time, overcome. Peirce emphasized not only the continuing nature of the process of inquiry but also what might be called the objective or communal nature of knowledge. These ideas seem to correspond with the central tenets of Holmes's jurisprudential theory. Holmes never acknowledged any debt to Peirce or for that matter to any one else. All we know is that, over a period of several years, both men attended meetings of a group at which these ideas were, in all probability, discussed.

In 1880 Holmes was approaching his fortieth year. He apparently believed that a man who does not have some great accomplishment to his credit before he is forty will never accomplish anything. For the better part of fifteen years he had been practicing law in Boston, without great success. He had prepared an edition of Kent's *Commentaries*[18] and had written a number of law review articles. But the great accomplishment had eluded him. At that point he was invited to deliver a series of lectures at the Lowell Institute in Boston. He seems to have looked on this opportunity as his last chance to meet his own deadline for greatness. He must have been pleased— or relieved—at the astonishing reaction to his lectures, both when they were delivered in November and December of 1880 and when they were published the following spring under the title *The Common Law*. Within a year a professorship had been established for him at Harvard which, much to the annoyance of his new Harvard colleagues, he almost immediately resigned to accept an appointment to the Supreme Judicial Court of Massachusetts. After his appointment to the bench Holmes never returned to the world of scholarship, so that the lectures in *The Common Law* remain as his only attempt to formulate a coherent, comprehensive statement of his theories about law.

The lectures have long since become unreadable unless the reader is prepared to put forward an almost superhuman effort of will to keep his attention from flagging and his interest from wandering. Our difficulty with the lectures may stem from the fact that they are not what they pretend to be.

They pretend to be a historical survey of the development of a few fundamental common law principles which, according to Holmes, had recurrently manifested themselves in the several fields he chose to deal with—principally criminal law, torts, and contracts. In fact, the historical underpinning was patently absurd, even when it had not been deliberately distorted. I do not mean to suggest that Holmes was a poor historian or that he did not know what he was doing. He was an excellent historian and knew more about what he was doing than most of us do. He was making a highly original, essentially philosophical statement about the nature of law. For reasons which he never explained, he chose to dress his statement in the misleading disguise of pseudo-history. Perhaps the disguise was a way of sugarcoating the pill—of making the new and unfamiliar appear to be old and familiar. Perhaps it was an elaborate joke which it amused Holmes, who was of a sardonic turn of mind, to play on his audience.[19]

Our difficulty with the lectures may also relate to unresolved tensions in Holmes's thought. For one example, Holmes seems to have looked on the aggregate of legal doctrine at any given time and place as an unstable mass characterized by internal inconsistency. Toward the end of his first lecture he generalized his views on the necessary instability and inconsistency of any given state of the law:

> What has been said will explain the failure of all theories which consider the law only from its formal side, whether they attempt to deduce the *corpus* from *a priori* postulates, or fall into the humbler error of supposing the science of the law to reside in the *elegantia juris,* or logical cohesion of part with part. The truth is, that the law is always approaching, and never reaching, consistency. It is forever adopting new principles from

life at one end, and it always retains old ones from history at the other, which have not yet been absorbed or
sloughed off. It will become entirely consistent only
when it ceases to grow.[20]

The trouble is that Holmes failed to keep in mind his own
profound insight into the complex interplay between new
materials drawn from life and old materials from the past
which have not yet been sloughed off. He talks to us from
on high, laying down principles of unrestricted universality,
reducing the bases of liability to what he called, in one of
the lectures on torts, a "philosophically continuous series."[21]
On the face of things he purports to be making a purely descriptive statement about what the law is here and now—in
Massachusetts in 1880—together with an account of how,
historically, it came to be that way. But most of the time he
is in fact making prescriptive statements about what the law
ought to be—at all times and in all places.

The basic hypothesis in Holmes's attempt to reduce all
theories of liability to a "philosophically continuous series"
was one which, so far as I know, had no antecedents in the
jurisprudential literature. Holmes hypothesized that the
progress of the law—or of legal rules—is always toward an
ideal state (which will never be reached) in which liability,
both civil and criminal, will be governed by formal, external,
and objective standards. In primitive legal systems, liability
depends on the defendant's subjective state of mind, his intent to cause harm, or, at the least, on his having become the
instrumentality through which harm is accomplished. A legal system approaches maturity to the extent that it succeeds
in eliminating any reference to what the defendant actually
thought, intended, or willed. In a mature system the defendant's conduct will be judged in the light of the general stan-

dards accepted in the relevant community; individual guilt or moral blameworthiness become alike irrelevant. The good man and the bad man stand equal at the bar of justice.

Holmes, wisely, never attempted to demonstrate the historical truth of his hypothesis. He seems to have thought of his hypothetical course of development—from moral, internal, subjective to amoral, external, objective—as a slow-moving glacier whose visible progress can be measured only in centuries. A startling aspect of his lectures is the repeated insistence that the principles of liability appropriate to the late nineteenth-century United States had been laid down in the English yearbooks of the fourteenth and fifteenth centuries. Most people had misunderstood what the old cases were about, principally because they had been misled by lapses into a moralistic terminology. But, with Holmes to set the record straight, it soon becomes crystal-clear that there is really no difference between a landowner in the reign of Edward IV who allowed thorns to fall onto his neighbor's land and a nineteenth-century railroad corporation whose spark-emitting engines caused damage to property adjacent to the right-of-way.

The problem to which Holmes addressed himself might be phrased thus: under what circumstances and to what extent should A be liable to B for damage or loss which B has suffered as a result of whatever it is that A has done or said or represented or promised? Holmes's answer was clear-cut: over the broadest possible range A should not be held to any liability at all; even when his liability must be conceded, the damages to be assessed against him must be kept to a minimum. These ideas, which are constantly reiterated throughout the lectures, receive their clearest expression in the course of the first lecture on torts. Holmes devoted a lengthy passage to a refutation first of Austin's view that liability was based on disobedience to the sovereign's command—thus on personal fault—and then of a view which he described as having been "adopted by some of the greatest common-law authorities" (none of whom is named) which was that "under the common law a man acts at his peril." Having disposed of his straw men Holmes continued:

> The general principle of our law is that loss from accident must lie where it falls, and this principle is not affected by the fact that a human being is the instrument of misfortune. . . .
>
> A man need not, it is true, do this or that act—the term *act* implies a choice—but he must act somehow. Furthermore, the public generally profits by individual activity. As action cannot be avoided, and tends to the public good, there is obviously no policy in throwing the hazard of what is at once desirable and inevitable upon the actor.[22]

It is by no means clear what the link in Holmes's mind was between his hypothesis about the progress of the law toward externality and objectivity and his conclusion about the desirability of restricting or denying liability for the incidentally harmful consequences of socially useful activity. He may have hypothesized that the increasing technological complexity of civilization required an increasingly wide range of privileged activity. But the link, whatever it may have been, remained implicit; nothing in Holmes's own writing, scholarly or judicial, ever clarified the matter.

I have taken Langdell and Holmes as twin symbols of the new age, which I have called the Age of Faith. Langdell's thought was crude and simplistic. Holmes's thought was subtle, sophisticated, and, in the last analysis, highly ambiguous.

Holmes's accomplishment was to make Langdellianism intellectually respectable. He provided an apparently convincing
demonstration that it was possible, on a high level of intellectual discourse, to reduce all principles of liability to a single,
philosophically continuous series and to construct a unitary
theory which would explain all conceivable single instances
and thus make it unnecessary to look with any particularity
at what was actually going on in the real world. Langdellian
jurisprudence and Holmesian jurisprudence were like the
parallel lines which have arrived at infinity and have met.

III

In the academic world the influence of the two men was
direct and immediate, consciously perceived and universally
acknowledged. And the American law school, in the new
format which Langdell had designed, became a principal in-
strument in the process of restructuring our jurisprudential
thought and reshaping our legal system.[23]

The great age of the American law school has long since
passed and will never come again. It may well be that no educational institutions in any country at any time have enjoyed
the prestige and achieved the success of the dozen or so national law schools which grew up in the image of Langdell's
Harvard. To be accepted as a student—or at all events to
survive the cut at the end of the first year—at one of these
schools was a guaranty of success. To be a professor of law
on one of the great faculties was to hold a passport to fame
and fortune.

Until Langdell's time the typical law professor had been
a retired practitioner or judge—like Chancellor Kent—or a
part-time instructor who devoted the bulk of his time and
energy to other pursuits. Langdell recruited his faculty from

recent graduates of the law school who had never practiced
law and had no intention of ever doing so; they were expected
to devote their full time to teaching and writing. These young
men, given tenure in their twenties, sensibly responded, in
an astonishing number of cases, by living into their nineties;
pre-retirement tenures approaching fifty years were not uncommon. That the courses in contracts, torts, or what not
were still being taught in the 1920s by professors who had
joined the faculty in the 1880s gave a remarkable continuity
to the educational process.

The law schools exerted their influence in two ways. One
was the contact between professor and student in classroom,
office, or law library. One of the good things about Langdell's
reform was that the members of the law faculty spent—and
even today continue to spend—much more of their time
teaching and talking to students than the members of any
other graduate faculty in any university would consider tolerable. The impact of this intense relationship between a distinguished faculty and a gifted student body seems to have
been, over a long period, enormous. After your three years in
Cambridge or wherever, you would never be the same again;
you were stamped, branded, brainwashed for life. And the
graduates of the national law schools, whether they returned
to their own states or joined the new-style large law firms in
New York or Boston or Philadelphia or Chicago, went on, in
disproportionate numbers, to become the leaders of bar and
bench in their successive generations.

The other way in which the law schools made their presence felt was through the production of a new type of legal
literature. The new academic literature would have made its
appearance in any case, following the success of Langdell's
reform. The form which the literature took seems, however,
to have been determined by an event which had nothing to

do with Langdell, legal education, or jurisprudential theory. I refer to the establishment of the National Reporter System by the West Publishing Company during the 1880s.[24] Now, for the first time, all the decisions, not only of the federal appellate courts but of all the state courts of last resort, were made available to lawyers throughout the country. Being available, they had to be used: even a middle-sized law firm in a middle-sized city could not afford to be without a full set of reports. And, as we know to our sorrow, the number of volumes published increased year by year in geometric progression.

The West Publishing Company, whose interest in juris-prudential theory I assume to have been minimal, thus made a contribution to our legal history which, in its importance, may have dwarfed the contributions of Langdell, Holmes, and all the learned professors on all the great law faculties. After ten or fifteen years of life with the National Reporter System, the American legal profession found itself in a situa-tion of unprecedented difficulty. There were simply too many cases, and each year added its frightening harvest to the ap-palling glut. A precedent-based, largely non-statutory system could not long continue to operate under such pressures.

The new generation of Langdell-trained law professors ar-rived just as the situation was becoming intolerable. Fortu-nately, one of the basic tenets of Langdellian jurisprudence provided the perfect remedy. That was the proposition that "the vast majority [of cases]—are worse than useless, for any purpose of systematic study."[25] The earlier practitioner-oriented literature had served to draw the reader's atten-tion to what cases there were. A principal function of the new academic literature was to draw the line between the correct cases and the vast majority of worthless ones. The string citations of the wrongly decided cases, which are to be disregarded, not infrequently outnumbered the parallel strings of correct cases. The new writers also followed the fashion, which Langdell had introduced, of using English rather than American cases as leading authorities; the lead citation in the ritual footnote collecting the correct cases was, almost invariably, an English case. A third feature of the new literature was its quality of bloodless abstraction. The facts of cases were rarely stated in any detail and were almost never analyzed. The customary procedure was to state the correct rule, often in black-letter text, and then proceed to justify it in terms of high-level generalities. The supporting cases came in at the bottom of the page in typically factless string citations.

It is easy to make fun of the Langdellian literature, which seems to us to have been overgeneralized and overconceptualized to a laughable degree. But we should also remember that the treatises and the law review articles represented a massive intellectual achievement. I have suggested that the new literature can be taken as a response to the pressures generated by the floods and torrents of published case reports. It is hard to see how the system could have continued to operate even tolerably well without the simplification and purification of doctrine which the system-builders proposed.

IV

We have been talking at length about the law schools and their contribution in the post–Civil War period. How should we characterize the judicial product during the same period? While the professors were constructing their reductionist theories, what were the judges doing?

The few people—including myself—who have ever spent much time studying the judicial product of the period have been appalled by what they found.[26]

The tradition of judicial creativity does seem to have survived to some degree in the federal courts. There is no point in speculating on whether the federal judges were better qualified than the state judges. If we look at the problem institutionally, it may be that the federal courts continued to benefit from the doctrine of *Swift* v. *Tyson* and the relaxed view toward precedent which that case counseled.[27] During this period the federal courts, proceeding without statutory warrant, invented the equity receivership for the reorganization of insolvent corporations—a remarkable instance of an innovative judicial response to an unprecedented economic situation.[28] Even in the federal courts, however, the pace slackens as we come down to the turn of the century. After 1900 the Supreme Court withdrew from the decision of private law questions and became a forum for the resolution of political controversies dressed up as issues of constitutional law. Without the Supreme Court to superintend, coordinate, and synthesize, the federalizing—or nationalizing—principle of *Swift* v. *Tyson* became a headless monster, marked down for destruction by all right-thinking men.[29]

As the federal courts went out of the business of making new law, the state courts, of necessity, took their place. In the earlier period the state courts had been quite as innovative as the federal courts. Gibson of Pennsylvania, Shaw of Massachusetts, Kent in New York—and many others—were judges of preeminent stature who made law with all the enthusiasm of a Marshall or a Story.[30] But when, after the Civil War, the state courts came into their inheritance, the supply of great judges seemed, almost overnight, to vanish. Except for Holmes in Massachusetts, it is hard, even for someone who is familiar with the literature, to summon up the name of a single judge.

The judicial product of the period can fairly be described as Langdellianism in action. I do not mean to suggest that, at

least in the beginning, the judges were consciously following
or adopting or copying Dean Langdell's theories. The truth
must have been the other way around. Langdell had intuitively sensed that the Civil War marked a watershed in our legal history, as it did in our political history, that a new age had
dawned, that a new approach to law had already come into
being. Langdell had nothing to do with creating the new age
or with shaping the new approach. He was, however, the first
to give a conscious, theoretical expression to the new order of
things—which is why he became the symbol of his time.

The post–Civil War judicial product seems to start from
the assumption that the law is a closed, logical system. Judges
do not make law: they merely declare the law which, in some
Platonic sense, already exists. The judicial function has nothing to do with the adaptation of rules of law to changing conditions; it is restricted to the discovery of what the true rules
of law are and indeed always have been. Past error can be exposed and in that way minor corrections can be made, but the
truth, once arrived at, is immutable and eternal. Change can
only be legislative and even legislative change will be treated
with a wary and hostile distrust. A statute in derogation of
the common law—as what statute is not?[31]—will be strictly
construed even if it cannot be set aside on constitutional
grounds as beyond the power of the legislature to enact.

This predisposition of the judges reflected itself in the
style of opinion-writing which came into vogue. This became
the age of the string citation—quite as much in the judicial
opinions as in the learned treatises. And the judges, like the
professors, rarely, if ever, bothered with the facts of the cases
they cited or with the reasons why the cases had been decided as they had been. Nor did the judges make any attempt
to explain the reasons for their decisions. It was enough to
say: The rule which we apply has long been settled in this

state (citing cases). Indeed, it was improper, unfitting, unjudicial to say more. The juice of life had been squeezed out; the case reports became so many dry husks. Stare decisis reigned supreme.[32]

The judges who thought this way and wrote this way set their faces against change. During this period the courts became the apostles of reaction and the guardians of a romanticized, oversimplified past. It is highly appropriate that the problems of labor organization and of industrial accidents long continued to be dealt with as parts of the law of master and servant—a turn of phrase which helped greatly to soften and blur the grim reality of life in, say, a steel mill in Pittsburgh or Gary. The legislatures, stirred by populist discontents, experimented with social legislation—regulating the hours and conditions of employment, restricting the exploitation of women and children, and so on. The courts routinely struck down these statutes on one or another ground—the most amusing ground having been the great principle of freedom of contract. That is to say, if a ten year old child wants to work twelve hours a day in a textile mill, by what warrant is the legislature empowered to deprive the child's parents of their right to enter into such a contract on his behalf? This attitude toward social legislation entrenched itself in the Supreme Court of the United States where, over the dissents of Holmes and Brandeis, it continued to command a majority long after the state courts had abandoned their root-and-branch opposition to anything new.[33]

V

Why should all of this—indeed, why should any of this—have happened?

It may be that every legal system, at some point in its development, goes through its Age of Faith. Sooner or later a

Blackstone or a Langdell appears. The idea of a body of law, fixed for all time and invested with an almost supernatural authority, is irresistibly attractive—not only for lawyers and their clients but, perhaps even more, for the populace at large. If a Blackstone or a Langdell comes at the right time, he will be heard and his words will, for a generation, be devoutly believed: his message is a comforting one and ought to be true even if it is not.

Since Langdell was heard and was believed, he evidently came at the right time. The fact that it took the English seven hundred years to produce their Blackstone while we produced our Langdell in seventy years merely serves to underline the accelerating tempo of life from the eleventh century to the nineteenth. By Langdell's time we had put behind us the problems which had concerned Kent and Story: how the common law of England should be adapted to the conditions of life in the United States, how a reasonable degree of national uniformity in the substantive law could be achieved in a decentralized federal republic.[34] We had accumulated a respectable number of our own precedents and, in addition, we had the English reports to draw on. The building materials were there; all we needed was someone to tell us how to go about putting them together.

The circumstances of life in the post–Civil War United States contributed to the success of Langdell's mission. After the terrible convulsion of the war we were in need of peace, repose, and tranquility: our energies as a nation were spent. Our politics degenerated into a sort of mush with two indistinguishable parties offering indistinguishable candidates to choose between. Our anarchists and militants were so far outside the mainstream of popular thought that only the unhappy victims of their assassination attempts had anything to fear from them.

The pace of technological progress slowed during this period. Anyone born in 1800 who lived until 1860 experienced the shock of technological change. Anyone born in 1850 who lived until 1910 experienced relatively little change except for the addition, toward the end of the period, of a few amenities like central heating and indoor plumbing. The great inventions which have unsettled our own lives did not have their impact until much later. Rapid technological change unsettles the law quite as much as it unsettles people. The slow pace of change during the half century after the Civil War contributed to the illusion that a stable body of law was not only a theoretical possibility but an accomplished fact.

The post–Civil War period saw the emergence of large-scale business enterprises, along with the vast fortunes which they generated. Undreamed-of aggregates of capital presented unheard-of problems for solution. The traditional bias of liberal theory in favor of the least possible governmental intervention—that government is best which governs least—made a sort of nonsense when you had to factor the railroads, the Standard Oil Trust, and United States Steel into the equation. On the other hand, laissez-faire economics had an obvious appeal to the movers and shapers of our economy. The theoretical structure which would leave the masters of the new wealth free to do their own thing in their own way was promptly provided. There has always been a symbiotic relationship between the academic establishment, which provides the theories, and the economic establishment, which appreciates being told that the relentless pursuit of private gain is the best way of serving the public interest.

In recent years it has become a truism to point out that laissez-faire economics and late nineteenth-century legal theories are blood brothers.[35] The hostility which the courts showed toward social legislation was a merely superficial manifestation of this relationship. On a deeper level the legal theorists who preached the doctrines of limited liability—the loss must lie where it falls—and of the lowest possible damages shared a community of interest with their economic counterparts who preached the religion of laissez-faire. And the quality of abstraction which came to characterize most legal writing seems like the mirror image of the idealized models of the economists. Even the economists must have felt a grudging admiration for the lawyers who could see that the case of a workingman bargaining with his corporate employer over wages and the case of a Vermont farmer dickering with a summer resident over the price of a cord of firewood could both be reduced to the paradigm of A who voluntarily contracts with B.

I have credited Holmes with the original formulation of most of these theories—although I should add that Holmes never shared the prevalent hostility toward social legislation. Holmes had no great sympathy for such legislation—he thought that most of it was silly and useless—but he consistently maintained his position that the dominant political majority is entitled to work its will on its defeated adversaries.[36] The other ideas all seem to have come from Holmes. Like Langdell before him, Holmes had intuitively sensed the felt necessities of the time and had succeeded in giving a magisterial expression to apparently revolutionary ideas which had, unnoticed, already worked their way into the common law. The stalwarts of the post–Holmesian orthodoxy took from the master only what suited them; the disturbing and heretical aspects of his thought were ignored.

4

The Age of Anxiety

I

All Ages of Faith may well be of brief duration. The pleasant and comforting myth of the law's internal consistency and external stability cannot, for long, sustain itself. The facts of life cannot, for long, be suppressed. Every Blackstone must have his Bentham; every Langdell must have his Llewellyn. The specifics of the breakdown, like the specifics of the original construction, are determined by the accidents of time and place.

From the vantage point of the 1970s it is clear enough that the great structure of Langdellian jurisprudence crumbled during the period between the two World Wars. It did not, of course, come tumbling down all at once like the walls of Jericho at Joshua's trumpet-blast. And the truth of the matter may be that the spirit of Langdellianism survived the apparent rout of the Langdellian forces during the bitter jurisprudential battles of the 1920s and 1930s—just as the spirit of Rome may be said to have survived the collapse of empire to reappear in the guise of the Catholic church.[1] But even if, for the sake of the argument, we concede the identity of the two Romes, we may go on to observe that the style and trappings of Catholic Rome were quite different from the style and trappings of Imperial Rome. We can be equally sure that a revivified and resurgent Langdellianism would bear little outward resemblance to the original.[2]

The most extraordinary aspect of our Age of Faith seems to me to have been the universality of a shared belief, the absence of dissent, the politeness of debate with an opposition whose proudest boast was its loyalty, the power of the reigning establishment to charm its natural opponents into conformity. Thus Louis Dembitz Brandeis, a Jewish lawyer from Kentucky with populist sympathies, could have a sensationally successful career at the Boston bar.[3] Thus Roscoe Pound, a reformed botanist from Nebraska who had advocated what was then called sociological jurisprudence, could become dean of the Harvard Law School.[4] Thus the progressives, who in a later generation would style themselves liberals, could outdo the conservatives in their fervent attachment to the American dream.[5] Reform, in those happy days, meant building up, not tearing down.

After 1900 the Langdellians themselves became reformers. The American codification movement had apparently died about the time of the Civil War; nothing had been heard from or about it since then.[6] In the 1890s the American Bar Association set up an affiliate or subsidiary which it called the National Conference of Commissioners on Uniform State Laws. The Conference went to work on a series of statutes designed to codify various aspects of commercial law, which had always been the preferred area of operation of the proponents of codification. Within a twenty-year period half a dozen statutes, of which the most important were the Negotiable Instruments Law and the Uniform Sales Act, had been drafted, promulgated, and widely enacted.[7] The presence of the American Bar Association as an approving sponsor makes clear that the codifying statutes were not the work of wild-eyed revolutionaries. But why should codification suddenly have become respectable?

Langdellian jurisprudence had been an attempt to achieve unity of doctrine on the case-law level.[8] Langdell and his followers were common lawyers to a man. The "one true rule of law" idea had been almost immediately subjected to intolerable pressures by the mounting flood of case reports. The writers of the great treatises sought to keep the situation under control by carefully distinguishing between the relatively few correct cases (many of them English) and the great piles of trash which filled the bound volumes of the reports. However another aspect of our late nineteenth-century theory caused trouble at exactly this point. Judges were not supposed to make law; they merely followed precedents. So, what was a judge who took the stare decisis business seriously—as many did—supposed to do when it turned out that the precedents in his state were, according to the learned gentlemen from Cambridge, wrong? The disunity of American case law from state to state may indeed have increased during the latter part of the nineteenth century as the nationalizing principle of *Swift v. Tyson* lost its strength. The *Swift v. Tyson* device had not infrequently succeeded in producing nationally acceptable solutions to regionally controverted issues.[9] As that device passed out of use, American case law apparently faced a bleak future of rampant parochialism.

American interest in codification had been stimulated by then recent English developments. The English, on their home turf, had paid not the slightest attention to Jeremy Bentham's strident manifestos calling for universal codification. The Benthamite idea was more attractive when the question became how best to secure the benefits of English civilization—including English law—for India. At all events, the English undertook and patiently carried out the ambitious project of providing India with English-inspired codes. The success of the Indian project led to a hesitant beginning in codifying some of the more troublesome areas of domestic law with the Bills of Exchange Act (1882) and the Sale of Goods Act (1893). Having gone so far, the English stopped and proceeded no further. Their two Victorian codifying statutes are still in effect. Proposals for further codification in this century have, after a flurry of initial publicity, been quietly abandoned.[10]

The American codifiers seem to have assumed that their function was to free judges, crippled by their devotion to stare decisis, from the fetters of aberrant precedents in un-enlightened jurisdictions. Indeed, the only truly enlightened jurisdiction was what was referred to in moot court competitions at the Harvard Law School as the State of Ames.[11] But with the law of Ames made available to all in statutory form, the true light could shine everywhere.

Statutes like the Uniform Sales Act were not statutes at all. That is, they were not designed to provide rules for decision. Drafted in terms of loose and vague generality, they were designed to provide access to the prevailing academic wisdom. The rules for decision in sales cases were to be found, not in the Uniform Sales Act which had been drafted by Samuel Williston of the Harvard Law School, but in Professor Williston's treatise on the law of sales.[12] This aspect of the codification was, apparently, generally understood. The courts—and counsel—paid no attention at all to the Sales Act; they paid enormous attention to Professor Williston's treatise. What we had was not so much a codification as a non-codification—a method of preserving the common law purged of all impurities.

The idea that the early twentieth-century codifiers were interested in common law preservation rather than statutory reform smacks of paradox. The idea, however, becomes less paradoxical in the light of the next major law reform project, which was undertaken in the 1920s and which enlisted the support of the groups which had earlier supported the uniform statutes. The American Law Institute, whose membership included the most distinguished lawyers, judges, and law professors of the time, was founded for the purpose of preparing a series of authoritative statements—which for some reason were called Restatements—of the principal branches of the common law: contracts, torts, agency, trusts, property, and so on.[13]

The Restatements, although cast in statutory form, were not designed to be (and were not) enacted as statutes by any legislature. The idea or the hope was that the Restatement formulations would exert a persuasive, even a compelling, force in purging the common law of eccentricities which might have arisen in particular jurisdictions and in promoting a soundly based uniformity throughout the country. The Restatements can be taken as a more direct method of achieving the same results which, earlier in the century, had been pursued through codification of the commercial law. Samuel Williston, who, following the success of the Sales Act, had become the quasi-official draftsman for the National Conference of Commissioners on Uniform States Laws, became the Chief Reporter for the American Law Institute's *Restatement of Contracts.*

There were a great many unresolved ambiguities about the Restatement project. Were the Restaters supposed to be "codifying" the law as it was? In situations where conflicting rules had evolved, were they supposed always to choose the "majority rule" over the "minority rule"? If a common law rule was felt to be unsatisfactory or unjust, were they at liberty to "restate" a "better rule" as determined by the membership of the Institute? If the law appeared, at the time of drafting, to be changing—with an old rule being abandoned and a different rule in course of being formulated—what were they supposed to do about that? The official position of the Institute on such issues was purely Langdellian: there were such things as the fundamental principles of the common law, which did not change; those principles, or most of them, were known, having been set out in the treatises which had proliferated for fifty years past; those principles (and not idiosyncratic cases) were the subject matter of the Restatements. No doubt most of the people who were caught up in the Restatement project shared the Institute's official position.

Blackstone's *Commentaries,* which advocated the preservation of English law without change, were written at a time when English law was undergoing violent, rapid, and fundamental change.[14] We can now see that, from the 1920s on, American law was entering into a period of comparable change. The Restatements, like the *Commentaries,* may be taken as the reaction of a conservative establishment, eager to preserve a threatened status quo. Like the *Commentaries,* the Restatements were applauded by most right-thinking men and may, for a time, have served their purpose.

The *Digest of Justinian* had collected, for the use of sixth-century Byzantium, the wisdom of third-century Roman jurisprudence. Not since the *Digest* had there been anything quite like the American Restatements. The fate of both these extraordinary legal artifacts was the same: the hurricane continued to howl; the foundations continued to slip away; the wisdom of the past could not save.[15]

We may take the provision in successive generations of the commercial law codifying statutes (which were not really statutes) and of the Restatements (which were merely a better expression of the same idea) as having obscurely reflected a realization on the part of the Langdellians—who enthusiastically supported both ventures—that things were not going as they were supposed to go, as for a generation or more they had appeared to be going.

II

Our dawning Age of Anxiety is perfectly symbolized by the mysterious—the almost mystical—figure of Benjamin Nathan Cardozo.[16] Cardozo's father had been a corrupt lower court judge allied with the Tweed Ring in New York, who had suffered disgrace when Tweed's organization was broken up. The son apparently felt that his mission was to redeem his father's sins. Ascetic in his personal tastes, he decided at an early age to renounce the pleasures and temptations of the world in favor of a life of intellectual meditation. The accounts of all those who knew him tell us of a man of compelling personal charm as well as of great sweetness of character. By the unanimous testimony of his contemporaries, Cardozo was a saint.[17]

Before his appointment to the Supreme Court of the United States in succession to Holmes, Cardozo served for nearly twenty years on the New York Court of Appeals and evidently dominated that great court, intellectually, throughout his tenure. Cardozo was a truly innovative judge of a type which had long since gone out of fashion. In his opinions, however, he was accustomed to hide his light under a bushel. The more innovative the decision to which he had persuaded his brethren on the court, the more his opinion strained to prove that no novelty—not the slightest departure from prior law—was involved. Since Cardozo was one of the best case lawyers who ever lived, the proof was invariably marshalled with a masterly elegance. It is not until the reader gets to the occasional angry dissent that he realizes that Cardozo had been turning the law of New York upside down.[18] During his twenty years Cardozo succeeded to an extraordinary degree in freeing up—and, of course, unsettling—the law of New York. It is true that he went about doing this in such an elliptical, convoluted, at times incomprehensible, fashion that the less gifted lower court New York judges were frequently at a loss to understand what they were being told.[19]

In 1920 Cardozo delivered a series of Storrs Lectures at the Yale Law School. Holmes's *The Common Law* and Cardozo's *The Nature of the Judicial Process* (the title under which his Yale lectures were published) are the two most celebrated books in the history of American jurisprudence.[20] The two books, however, have nothing in common beyond the facts that nobody reads them and everybody praises them.

Cardozo's book, as a matter of strict fact, has almost no intellectual content. He addressed himself to the problem of how a judge goes about deciding a case. In the great majority of all cases, he said, the outcome is foredoomed; the past has foreclosed the present. Only in an occasional case does the process of adjudication involve a creative act on the part of the judge. In such a case, Cardozo suggested, the judge may—indeed must—look to what he called the "methods" of philosophy, history, tradition, and sociology. By the "method of sociology" he meant that the judge, at least in a situation where he finds nothing else to guide him, is to take into account the effect of his decision on social or economic conditions.[21] Toward the end of his last lecture he introduced what might be called the theme of judicial anguish:

> I was much troubled in spirit, in my first years on the bench, to find how trackless was the ocean on which I had embarked. I sought for certainty. I was oppressed and disheartened when I found that the quest for it was futile. I was trying to reach land, the solid land of fixed and settled rules, the paradise of a justice that would declare itself by tokens plainer and more commanding than its pale and glimmering reflections in my own

vacillating mind and conscience. . . . As the years have
gone by, and as I have reflected more and more upon
the nature of the judicial process, I have become recon-
ciled to the uncertainty, because I have grown to see it
as inevitable. I have grown to see that the process in its
highest reaches is not discovery, but creation; and that
the doubts and misgivings, the hopes and fears, are part
of the travail of mind, the pangs of death and the pangs
of birth, in which principles that have served their day
expire, and new principles are born.[22]

The thing that is hardest to understand about *The Na-*
ture of the Judicial Process is the furor which its publication
caused. Nothing can better illustrate the extraordinary hold
which the Langdellian concept of law had acquired, not only
on the legal but on the popular mind. Cardozo's hesitant confession that judges were, on rare occasions, more than simple
automata, that they made law instead of merely declaring it,
was widely regarded as a legal version of hardcore pornog-
raphy. By this unseemly indiscretion, it was suggested, Cardozo had forfeited any claim he might otherwise have had
to be considered as a fit candidate for a seat on the Supreme
Court of the United States. In time the furor abated and he
took his seat on the Supreme Court without any visible sign
of public indignation. But a less saintly man than Cardozo
might, in 1920, have found himself running close to the reefs
of impeachment.[23]

Cardozo was, we might say, a revolutionary *malgré lui*
who was affectionately attached to the structure which, im-
perceptibly, almost surreptitiously, he proceeded to subvert
and destroy. There was however, nothing affectionate, imper-
ceptible, or surreptitious about the procedures of the group,
based mostly in the law schools, who came to be known as

the Legal Realists. They appeared to be in favor of tearing everything down. On further analysis the case may prove to be that, just as Cardozo was a revolutionary *malgré lui,* the Realists were Langdellians *malgré eux.* In times of revolutionary change, it is hard to tell who is on which side.

What the curious episode which we call American Legal Realism was about has long been a puzzle not only to outsiders but to the participants. Karl Llewellyn, whom most people regarded as the leading Realist, insisted throughout his life that there had never been a Realist "school" or a Realist "movement." Professor William Twining, one of the few English scholars who has studied our transatlantic law-ways, seems to have concluded, in a recent book on Llewellyn and the Realist Movement, that Legal Realism, if there was such a thing, was an exclusively American phenomenon which bore no relationship to any developments, past or present, in any other legal system.[24] Indeed Professor Twining suggests, by implication, that Legal Realism was, so to say, a play-off for the Ivy League championship, with the combined faculties of the Columbia and Yale Law Schools taking the field against Harvard. There was more to it than that.

In a narrow sense, the Realist controversy consisted of a series of articles which appeared in the law reviews during the 1930s and which, today, makes up as dreary a course of reading as anyone can hope to find anywhere.[25] When Llewellyn denied that there had ever been a Realist school or movement, he was, presumably, referring to the law review controversy. On the law review level, the issues at stake, which had never been clearly defined, became progressively more confused and more insubstantial as the debate went on. But neither Llewellyn nor anyone else ever denied that a fundamental shift in American legal thought had taken place in the decades following World War I.[26]

The one thing on which the academic theorists who emerged after World War I agreed was that the traditional or Langdellian way of achieving doctrinal unity on the level of case law or Restatement was absurd. However, in demonstrating the absurdity, the new generation of theorists used as their principal weapon one which Langdell himself had provided: the idea that the reported cases are the laboratory materials for our systematic or scientific study.[27] In its Langdellian version that had meant that we were to study a few correct cases and disregard the rest. The post-Langdellians proposed to look at all the cases.

Arthur Corbin may have been the first, as he was the greatest, of the post–Langdellian scholars.[28] Corbin took no part in the Realist controversy; in any event, his intellectual formation had been complete long before World War I. Llewellyn, who had studied under Corbin and had been closely associated with him, regarded Corbin as his spiritual father in the law. Indeed, all the Realists treated Corbin with a respect which they showed to almost no other figure of his generation.

Corbin counseled not only that we should study all the cases but that we should study them not so much for their doctrinal statements as for what he liked to call their "operative facts." Furthermore, Corbin practiced what he preached, not only in his teaching but in his writings which culminated in his great treatise on contracts. In Corbin we no longer find the high-level generalities supported by factless string citations which had characterized the Langdellian literature, whose greatest achievement had been the other great treatise on contracts written by Corbin's dear friend and lifelong opponent, Samuel Williston.[29] In Corbin we find painstaking factual analyses of all the cases, even those of minor importance which are relegated to the footnotes. Indeed the practice

of paying an obsessive regard to the facts of cases, while dis-
regarding their doctrinal content, became after World War I,
and has since remained, a characteristic of most American
legal scholarship.

Unity of doctrine cannot survive that way of dealing with
cases. The process of disintegration is already evident in
Corbin's own work. In Anglo-American law it has, for several
centuries, been customary to say that contractual liability
will not be imposed on a promisor unless his promise is supported by something called consideration. Corbin concluded
that there is not, and never has been, such a thing as a, or the,
doctrine of consideration. At various times and in various
places and in a great variety of circumstances, courts have
imposed contractual liability. The only purpose of studying
the field is to determine under what circumstances the liability has been imposed. There is no harm, Corbin cheerfully
concluded, in using the word *consideration* which has been
bequeathed to us by history. But, he added, if you want to use
it, you should be aware that it means, and always has meant,
many different and inconsistent things.[30]

Some of those who followed in Corbin's footsteps carried his teaching to the point of intellectual nihilism. Wesley Sturges, whom generations of students at the Yale Law
School revered as the greatest of teachers, was one.[31] Early in
his career Sturges published a few law review articles which
were of an almost unbelievably narrow scope and focus—for
example, an elaborate study of the North Carolina case law
on the nature of mortgages, a subject of no conceivable interest to Sturges or anyone else.[32] The point of the study was to
demonstrate that the North Carolina law of mortgages made
no sense and could most charitably be described as a species
of collective insanity on the march. At about the same time
he put together a casebook for a new course which he called

Credit Transactions: the casebook consisted principally of the most absurd cases, along with the most idiotic law review comments, which he had been able to find.[33] The law, as Wesley Sturges conceived it, bore a striking resemblance to the more despairing novels of Franz Kafka. Sturges himself had the courage of his bleak convictions. *Ex nihilo nihil.* He wrote almost nothing during the remainder of his long career.[34] No one could match Sturges in his penetrating analysis of the most complex legal materials, but he saw no point in playing children's games. I was his student and served on his faculty while he was dean of the Yale Law School: he was a lonely, great, and tragic figure.

III

The process of disintegration of unitary theory and of return toward a pre-Langdellian pluralism, already apparent in Corbin's work, became even more marked in the work of Corbin's disciple, Karl Llewellyn.[35] In 1930 Llewellyn published a casebook on sales, which broke with tradition by including a great deal of analytical and historical material as well as by supplementing the leading cases reprinted in full with digests of hundreds, if not thousands, of related cases. He followed the casebook with a series of magisterial articles on sales law.[36] In both the articles and the casebook he traced, in meticulous detail, the development of sales law in the United States from the 1800s to his own time. Llewellyn's work in sales, like Corbin's work in contracts, was designed to prove that the apparent unity of the orthodox version of sales law (represented by Williston's treatise on sales and by the Uniform Sales Act which Williston had drafted) had been achieved by a serious distortion of historical fact and truth. Llewellyn, however, went well beyond Corbin in articulating his own theoretical position. The essential vice in the Willistonian construct, as Llewellyn saw it, was the attempt to derive all the rules of sales law from a few general principles, assumed to be universally applicable. The remedy lay in what Llewellyn referred to as "narrow issue thinking." Under Williston's Sales Act, for example, the remedies available on breach depended on whether seller or buyer owned ("had the property in") the goods at the time of the breach. The rules for determining when the property passed from seller to buyer became complicated, even metaphysical, but the threshold question in Sales Act litigation had to be the resolution of the property issue. Llewellyn's thesis was that the entire property concept should be scrapped along with the idea that all contracts of sale should be treated alike. Transactions between professionals (or merchants) should be treated differently from transactions in which a professional sold goods to a nonprofessional (or consumer). Sales for resale should be treated differently from sales for use. Distinctions should be made between sales for cash and sales on credit; present sales and future sales; one-shot or single delivery transactions and long-term contract arrangements. Llewellyn's atomization of sales law, like Corbin's atomization of contract law, was at the opposite pole from the Langdellian attempt to reduce all principles of liability to what Holmes had called a "philosophically continuous series."[37]

Llewellyn's chosen field was one which had already been codified. For that reason his articles were for the most part attacks on the Uniform Sales Act coupled with proposals that the Sales Act should be replaced with a statute which would reflect (as the Sales Act did not) the actual practices of businessmen in the twentieth century. It is rarely a reformer's lot to have the opportunity to carry out the reforms which he has advocated. Llewellyn did indeed become the principal

draftsman of what was initially known as the Uniform Revised Sales Act and later became the Uniform Commercial
Code. The Code (which is now in force in all American jurisdictions except Louisiana) was the most ambitious project of
law reform which has been carried out in this century. What
came out of the labors of Llewellyn and many others over the
better part of twenty years is the best example that can be
found of the confusions and crosscurrents of American law
during the protracted period of the Code's drafting.[38]

The Code was jointly sponsored by the National Conference of Commissioners on Uniform State Laws (which
had acquired a de facto monopoly of commercial law
codification)[39] and the American Law Institute (which had
completed the Restatement project[40] but was, like any organization, reluctant to shut up shop and go out of business).
The Conference had access to the state legislatures; the Institute had access to money; at the relevant time William
Schnader, a Philadelphia lawyer, held high office in both organizations and is credited with having arranged their unlikely collaboration. While the memberships overlapped to
some extent, the Conference was predominantly made up of
small-town lawyers; the typical Institute member was a senior partner in a prestigious law firm or a federal judge or a
law school dean. Most Commissioners and most members of
the Institute were conservatives—not only in politics but in
jurisprudence.

There is a comforting irony in the fact that the Conference and Institute not only chose Karl Llewellyn as principal draftsman (or Chief Reporter) for the Code but succeeded in living with him for fifteen years on terms of mutual
respect and amity. Llewellyn in the 1930s had become the
symbol of the academic revolt against Langdellianism and
orthodoxy. He was flamboyant both in his personality and

his prose style. He must have seemed, to most members of both Conference and Institute, unsound. On the other hand, Llewellyn had been a devoted member of the Conference for many years and had become the Conference's principal draftsman in commercial law matters.[41] He was also, beyond question, the preeminent academic authority on sales law (which was the starting point for the Code project): a revised Sales Act without Llewellyn's participation would have been as unthinkable as a *Restatement of Contracts* without Williston's. In all probability, Llewellyn thought that he could persuade his employers to adopt his own theories. In turn, the people who controlled the Conference and Institute thought that they could make use of Llewellyn's drafting skills and encyclopedic knowledge of the law, while reserving the power to veto any excesses toward which their unpredictable Chief Reporter might seek to lead them.

On the whole and in the long run the conservatives or traditionalists had their way. Llewellyn's proposals for a radical restructuring of the law—as, for example, in distinguishing between the standards applicable to "merchants" and those applicable to non-merchants—survived the early drafts only in an attenuated, watered down, almost meaningless form. Provisions which would have notably increased the liability of manufacturers for their defective goods were simply deleted from the later drafts. Not only the substance but the style of the Code changed dramatically as the drafting process continued. Llewellyn himself had had the concept of what he called a "case law code"—by which he meant a statute whose principal function would be to abrogate obsolete rules, thus leaving the courts free to improvise new rules to fit changing conditions and novel business practices. Llewellyn's code, as he conceived it, would have abolished the past without attempting to control the future. That jurisprudential approach did not satisfy the groups of practicing lawyers who participated in the project and whose influence increased as the drafting approached the final stages. These lawyers had perhaps become uneasily aware of mounting indications of a new style of judicial activism.[42] At all events they insisted on a tightly drawn statute, designed to control the courts and compel decision. To a considerable degree, they got what they wanted.

The Code in its final form can best be described as a compromise solution which satisfied no one. Llewellyn had recruited a drafting staff which was composed mostly of younger law professors whose own ideas about law had been greatly influenced by Llewellyn and the other Realists. Sharing Llewellyn's views, they produced drafts which reflected his own pluralism and anti-conceptualism. Those drafts were largely rewritten by practitioners whose instinctive approach to law was more conventional. Even so, the Code, as rewritten, retained more than mere traces of the earlier approach, both in substance and in style. It testifies to the fundamental cleavage which, by the 1940s, had overtaken the legal profession in this country.

It was the curious fate of the Code, a 1940s statute, not to have been widely enacted until the 1960s. In the 1950s the legal establishment which controlled the bar associations (and had great influence with the bankers' associations) opposed the Code and was successful in preventing its enactment. In the 1960s the same people who had fought the Code ten years earlier had reversed their field and were counted among its most vigorous supporters. A plausible reason for this reversal is that during the 1950s the courts, in a surge of activism, had themselves been rewriting much of the law. The Code, which in the 1940s had seemed much too "liberal" to its conservative critics, had by the 1960s become an almost nostalgic throwback to an earlier period. The final irony in the Code project was that its eventual "success" (that is, its enactment) can well be taken as an attempt by the most conservative elements in the bar to turn the clock back.

IV

At least in the law schools, the jurisprudential revolution had, by 1940 or thereabouts, won a complete success.[43] (And it should be borne in mind that what is taught in the law schools in one generation will be widely believed by the bar in the following generation.) The "conceptualism" of the Langdellian period was, by everyone except a few die-hard traditionalists, held up to scorn. The great treatises and the Restatements which had followed in their wake were pilloried as nonsensical attempts to portray the life of the law as having been logic rather than experience: it was assumed that the treatises would not (and should not) have any successors. The idea that the process of judicial decision was much more irrational than it was rational had a fashionable currency. With the solitary exception of Holmes, the theorists and system-builders of our vanished Age of Faith were caricatured as simpleminded reactionaries.

And yet the revolution may have been merely a palace revolution, not much more than a changing of the guard. My own thought has come to be that the adepts of the new jurisprudence—Legal Realists or whatever they should be called—no more proposed to abandon the basic tenets of Langdellian jurisprudence than the Protestant reformers of the fifteenth and sixteenth centuries proposed to abandon the basic tenets of Christian theology.[44] These were the ideas that "law is a science" and that there is such a thing as "the one true rule of law."

At the hands of the Realists, the slogan "law is a science" became "law is a social science." Where Langdell had talked of chemistry, physics, zoology, and botany as disciplines allied to the law,[45] the Realists talked of economics and sociology not merely as allied disciplines but as disciplines which were in some sense part and parcel of the law. Economists, sociologists, and even psychiatrists were invited to join the faculties of the major law schools and did so in considerable numbers. What were called non-legal materials began to appear in the casebooks, which themselves became "Cases and Materials" to indicate that studying law no longer meant studying the cases which, according to Langdell, were our "experimental materials."

Few lawyers ever bothered to study any of the social sciences (any more than the social scientists, even those who joined the law faculties, ever bothered to study law). But from the 1930s on, it became an article of faith for a great many lawyers and law professors that the social sciences had come much closer to the "truth" than traditional legal scholarship had ever done. The social scientists agreed with this flattering estimate of their work.

The work of such scholars as Corbin had popularized the idea that what counted in the law was not abstract doctrine but concrete facts. The fact-sensitivity to which American lawyers had been conditioned was, I suggest, one of the factors which accounted for their enthusiastic acceptance of the social science idea. The facts underlying a transaction or a business practice or a social custom can be glimpsed in judicial opinions only as through a glass darkly. The courts themselves, burdened by procedural limitations and restricted to adversary proceedings, are poor institutions for finding out what the essential facts are or were. The individual judge is a nonspecialist with respect to the economic or social background of the cases which come before him and is not supposed to go beyond the record made by counsel. Thus the inadequacy of judicial fact-finding techniques makes judicial opinions worthless as accounts of what is actually going on in the world.

It appeared, however, that the social scientists, particularly the sociologists, had made great advances in techniques of empirical research. If the law professors adopted those techniques, they could marshal the facts on which enlightened decision depends. Since the 1930s a great many empirical study projects on legal issues have been undertaken, typically funded by lavish foundation grants and publicized at well-attended press conferences. The fate of most of these projects has been to wither on the vine without producing any fruit. It is a fact of life that thinking or talking about doing empirical research is much more fun than actually doing it. And even if you have the resources to employ armies of research assistants to gather all the facts there are, the gathered facts have a disappointing way of turning out not to mean anything beyond themselves. However, despite the skeptical opinion which has just been expressed, research projects which can be described as "empirical" have been, and continue to be, popular both with university administrations and with foundations (which do have to find some way of spending their money).

The lawyers who became fact-gatherers and thought of themselves as social scientists had to provide themselves with sets of values or goals. These could be, and usually were, drawn from whichever of the "allied disciplines" an individual lawyer was familiar with: Keynesian (or anti-Keynesian or pseudo-Keynesian) economic theory, stimulus-response or Freudian psychology, current theories in vogue among anthropologists or sociologists, and so on. Myres McDougal (whose training had been in law) and Harold Lasswell (who had started his career as a political scientist) collaborated on the elaboration of a system of jurisprudence which they called policy science.[46] The central feature of the McDougal-Lasswell system was a set of basic values (such as wealth, power, rectitude, enlightenment, and so on) which were defined in terms of high-level generality. Developments in the law were to be analyzed and evaluated in the light of the basic values on which, it was assumed, all reasonable men would agree. Despite the novelty of its trappings, the work of McDougal and Lasswell, particularly in its insistence that everything can be reduced to a few general principles, can, not unfairly, be taken as a return toward older theories of law and as a reaction against the pluralism of such scholars as Corbin and Llewellyn.

A great deal of the legal writing which was published through the 1940s took on a political coloration which, before World War I, had been called progressive, then, somewhat later, liberal, and was finally associated with the New Deal of the 1930s. There were no doubt many reasons for the leftward-leaning political allegiance of the post-Langdellians, which in many individual instances may not have been a matter of deeply held conviction. In any case, the emerging patterns of post–World War I liberalism, which was destined to hold political power for a generation, were perfectly tailored to fit the preconceptions of Realist jurisprudence.

The Realists, who were deeply concerned with social and economic problems, had little use for the judicial process. The obvious alternative to a judicial solution of such problems is a legislative solution. A legislative committee, unlike a court, can analyze a problem in depth and cut through to a rational solution. If continuing supervision or regulation is required, an administrative agency which will quickly develop its own expertise is the answer. In the first flush of enthusiasm, doing all this seems like child's play. Jeremy Bentham seems to have believed that running up a comprehensive code for England, France, or the United States would be as easy as rolling off a log. In this country in the twentieth century we have had more than our fair share of Jeremy Benthams.

The idea of governmental intervention to improve the quality of life became the stock-in-trade of the progressive movement.[47] States which came under the influence of progressive ideology—Wisconsin under the LaFollettes, Pennsylvania under Gifford Pinchot—were hailed as laboratories for experiments in social progress. The possibility that the experiments might fail seems never to have been seriously considered. With the coming of the New Deal the opportunity for experimentation on a much grander scale was at hand. Many of the academic Realists, gladly forsaking their lives of scholarly research, enlisted for the duration and were among the leading movers and shakers of the New Deal period. They drafted statutes by the gross and set up administrative agencies by the score. Having created a new world, they rested and hallowed it. But the problems did not go away, and Utopia was as remote as ever. What to do about these mouldering statutes and elderly agencies will presently become an urgent problem of law reform.

V

While the legal scholars were becoming social scientists and the legal activists were drafting statutes and administering agencies, what were the judges doing? The conventional wisdom of the 1930s was that judicial power was a relic of the dead past. The Realists had stripped the judges of their trappings of black-robed infallibility and revealed them to be human beings whose decisions were motivated much more by irrational prejudice than by rules of law. The law, state and federal, was in process of being reduced to statutory form with most of the significant continuing problems being committed to administrative agencies. The judicial role was bound to become progressively more modest, more mechanical, more trivial. What happened, as is frequently the case, was the opposite of what the conventional wisdom assumed.

The activism of the Warren Court in areas of public or constitutional law has for a long time been a matter of public praise or blame. The truth is that the birth, or rebirth, of judicial activism considerably antedated the formation of the Warren Court and has been quite as much a factor to be reckoned with in the state courts as in the federal courts and in areas of private law as in areas of public law.[48] Present prospects are that this surge of activism will continue, no matter who may sit on the Supreme Court of the United States or on our less august tribunals.[49]

In an earlier chapter, I suggested that the post–Civil War judges and theorists seemed, on the obscure level of instinct, to be working toward the same goals.[50] The patterns which the theorists provided and the results which the judges arrived at were in perfect harmony. Characteristic of our post–Civil War jurisprudence was its fondness for abstraction and for building unitary theories as well as its insistence on restricting both liability and damages.

No doubt the obscure correspondence between theory and practice holds true in any period. It has surely been true in this century that the reforms which the professors called for in their law review articles were already being provided, or had been provided, by the judges, without anybody having noticed what had happened. The universal abstractions faded, the unitary theories disappeared, the range of liability became wider and wider and plaintiff's damages flourished like the green bay tree.[51]

The rebirth of judicial activism has gone hand in hand with a rebirth of the federalizing or nationalizing principle. In 1938 the Supreme Court declared that the federal law doctrine of *Swift* v. *Tyson* was, and always had been, unconstitutional.[52] The *Swift* v. *Tyson* device, which had over a long period been of great service, had ceased to work in this century. The only sensible course was to get rid of it, as the Supreme Court did. But, having scrapped the machine that no longer worked, the Court immediately set about providing a substitute that would work.

Even at the time the *Erie* case was decided, a prescient observer might have commented that the case's apparent meaning could hardly be taken as its true meaning. Control over the development of the substantive law was not going to be returned to the states at a time when the powers and presence of the federal government had reached a point unknown in our history. And that proposition, which was clearly enough true in the years preceding World War II, had long since passed the point of no return by the time we had come to the end of the war period.

The post-*Erie* federalization of the law was not established by the fiat of a single great case.[53] The federalizing principle has expressed itself in a variety of ways as the courts have reacted to the reality of ever-increasing federal power. Insofar as a principle has emerged, it is that the presence of any kind of federal interest in a case is enough to support the conclusion that decision should be governed by federal law rather than by the law of any state. Thus, contracts to which the United States, in any of its manifold capacities, is a party are contracts governed by federal law. The presence of a federal regulatory agency may lead to the conclusion that all the transactions in which the members of the regulated industry engage are governed by a uniform federal law to be supplied by the courts. It was once assumed as a matter of course that gaps in an incomplete federal statute were to be filled in in the light of principles borrowed from the common law—that is, the law of some state. That approach has been superseded by the idea that federal statutes generate a common law penumbra of their own: gaps are to be filled in by a process of extrapolation from whatever the court conceives the basic policy of the statute to be. Under the federal Constitution many areas of the law—admiralty, bankruptcy, and patents are obvious examples—are, in some sense, federal specialties. Nevertheless, until about the time of World War II the federal courts in deciding such cases routinely applied rules of state law in any situation where it did not appear that a specialized federal rule already existed. Since World War II the Supreme Court of the United States has given a wide currency to the ideas that, in federal specialty areas, a federal rule must be "fashioned" if one does not already exist and that a proper regard for federal supremacy requires the application of the federal rule even if the forum of litigation is a state court.[54] This aspect of the New Federalism goes well beyond the federal law doctrine of *Swift* v. *Tyson*. Under that doctrine federal courts were not bound by rules of state law, but state courts were under no duty to follow a federal rule.[55] Under the emerging federal supremacy doctrine, state courts will be bound by rules of federal law over an area which will itself grow as the powers of the federal government grow.

During the period when the apparent meaning of the *Erie* case was taken to be its true meaning, federal judges suffered much frustration when the state law rule by which, under *Erie,* they were bound turned out to be one which the state supreme court had announced fifty or seventy-five or a hundred years earlier and never since then reconsidered. The increasing localization of many types of litigation in the federal courts aggravated the problem. However, with the emergence of the federal rule-fashioning technique, no federal judge who has the slightest flair for his craft need any longer be concerned with even the most horrifying clinker which he may pick up from the nineteenth-century dustheap.

Between 1900 and 1950 the greater part of the substantive law, which before 1900 had been left to the judges for decision in the light of common law principles, was recast in statutory form. We are just beginning to face up to the consequences of this orgy of statute making. One of the facts of legislative life, at least in this country in this century, is that getting a statute enacted in the first place is much easier than getting the statute revised so that it will make sense in the light of changed conditions. On the federal level it is difficult to the point of impossibility to draw the attention of a crisis-ridden Congress to any area of law reform which, although it may be urgent, has not erupted in political controversy. And the more tightly a statute was drafted originally, the more difficult it becomes to adjust the statute to changing conditions without legislative revision.[56] Unfortunately, with the New Deal, a style of drafting which aimed at an unearthly and superhuman precision came into vogue, on the state as well as the federal level.

Eventually the problem of obsolescent statutes solves itself. No statutory draftsman has a crystal ball in which he can read the future. The best he can do is to make some kind of sense out of the recent past. A well-drafted statute will deal sensibly with the issues which have come into litigation during the twenty or twenty-five years which preceded the drafting. However, the focus of litigation has a way of shifting unexpectedly and unpredictably. New issues, which no one ever dreamed of, present themselves for decision. With luck, the statute will turn out to have nothing to say that is relevant to the new issues, which can then be decided on their own merits. In this way any statute gradually becomes irrelevant and will finally be reabsorbed within the mainstream of the common law. But that takes a long time.[57]

The most difficult period in the life of a statute—as in the life of a human being—is middle age. Admittedly the statute is no longer what it once was but there is life in the old dog yet. An occasional subsection still has its teeth and subparagraph (3)(b) may burn with a gem-like flame. We are now passing through our statutory middle age.

Statutory language—like any other kind of language— almost always presents alternative possibilities of construction. There will, however, be cases in which even the most disingenuous construction will not save the day. In such a case, it has always been assumed, a court must bow to the legislative command, however absurd, however unjust, however wicked. Once the legislature has taken over a field, only the legislature can effect any further change.

So far as my own knowledge takes me, it is only within the past ten or fifteen years that there have been suggestions in some judicial opinions to the effect that courts, faced with an obsolete statute and a history of legislative inaction, may take matters into their own hands and do whatever justice and good sense may seem to require. These suggestions have, for the most part, been put forward with an understandable degree of hesitant reluctance. As the idea becomes more familiar to us, I dare say that we will come to see that the reformulation of an obsolete statutory provision is quite as legitimately within judicial competence as the reformulation of an obsolete common law rule. Indeed, if we do not, we will presently find ourselves lost in a legal jungle with no hope of finding a way out.[58]

The New Federalism has largely freed us from the problem of obsolete judicial decisions on the state level. Obsolete decisions handed down long ago by the Supreme Court of the United States are coming to be a serious problem of obviously difficult solution. The Court, which is quite as crisis-ridden as Congress, is able to decide only a small fraction of the cases which are submitted to it. The energies of the Justices are taken up with grave issues of public order. Even if they had the time, they no longer have the expertise to deal with the issues of private law which, fifty or seventy-five years ago, accounted for a significant part of the Court's work. Since the Supreme Court will not, indeed cannot, reconsider many of its own arguably obsolete holdings, the time may have come for the inferior federal courts to experiment with the idea that, in case of need, they should not follow or consider themselves bound by obsolete Supreme Court cases—which would be a much cleaner approach to the problem than refined and artificial distinctions which lead only to states of intolerable complexity. In all probability, the worst fate that such innovative federal judges would have to fear would be reversal; it is unlikely that they would be impeached.[59]

5

On Looking Backward and Forward
at the Same Time

I

For two hundred years we have been in thrall to the eighteenth-century hypothesis that there are, in social behavior and in societal development, patterns which recur in the same way that they appear to recur in the physical universe.[1] If the hypothesis is sound, it must follow that, once the relevant developmental sequences which have led us to our present state have been correctly analyzed, we will know not only where we are but where we are going. Our understanding of the present will enable us to predict the future and, within limits, to control it. Once the forces at work are known, they can be channeled or harnessed to serve the needs and wants not necessarily of mankind at large but at least of those who are in a position to manipulate them.

We have never had to face up to that frightening possibility for the excellent reason that no historian, social scientist, or legal theorist has ever succeeded in predicting anything. After two hundred years of anguished labor, the great hypothesis has produced nothing. The formulations proposed in each generation have collapsed when the realities of the following generation have become known. Nevertheless, the dream dies hard. Each new generation of investigators has convinced itself that the cause of past failure lay in inadequate methodology and that, with more refined techniques, the trick will finally be pulled off. The historians continue to ransack the archives. The sociologists continue to perfect increasingly complicated ways of carrying on their empirical studies. It is true that some economists, having observed the fate of all the theories put forward by their predecessors, have succumbed to skepticism and seem ready to go out of the long-term prediction business.

One lesson which we can draw from all this is that the hypothesis is itself in error. Man's fate will forever elude the attempts of his intellect to understand it. The accidental variables which hedge us about effectively screen the future from our view. The quest for the laws which will explain the riddle of human behavior leads us not toward truth but toward the illusion of certainty, which is our curse. So far as we have been able to learn, there are no recurrent patterns in the course of human events; it is not possible to make scientific statements about history, sociology, economics—or law.

The assumption that we are engaged in an endeavor that can be properly described as scientific has clouded the vision and distorted the thinking of generations of legal scholars. The Legal Realists of the 1930s embraced the fallacy quite as enthusiastically as the Langdellian formalists.[2] As a group, the Realists unquestioningly accepted the idea of the "one true rule of law" which was waiting to be discovered if only the search was conducted in the right way. Realist jurisprudence proposed a change of course, not a change of goal.

The idea that "law is a science" has conditioned all our responses. It has dictated to us both what we were looking for and how we were to go about looking for it. If we can rid ourselves of the illusion that law is some kind of science—natural, social, or pseudo—and of the twin illusion that the purpose of law study is prediction, we shall be better off than we have been for at least a hundred years.

II

We took from the eighteenth century not only its belief in science but also its belief in the inevitability of progress. The two ideas are, indeed, closely linked. Science and progress go hand in hand. If we believe in science, we accept progress as its natural consequence. If we lose faith in the scientific method (at least as applied to social phenomena), we will also turn away from the belief in the perfectability of our society.

In the grisly aftermath of World War II the genial optimism which had for so long sustained us seems to have become, to many minds, no longer tenable or even tolerable. The dominant mood of our own bleak time may well have become a pervasive doubt or malaise, which easily modulates into a black despair at the human condition and its prospects.

One of the ways in which our twentieth-century despair has manifested itself has been in our changing attitudes toward the past. So long as we believe in ourselves, we look to the past (if we look to it at all) for instructive moral lessons designed to illustrate how and why everything necessarily works out for the best. When we cease to believe in ourselves, we look urgently to the past, not for instructive moral lessons, but in the desperate attempt to find out what went wrong. If only we could find that out, we instinctively feel, we could reverse our mistaken course and take whatever corrective measures might be necessary. Or, on a more reasoned level, we may feel that some understanding of our past mistakes may help us cope with our obscure present and unknown future. It is surely true that each generation gets the past it deserves. The fall of Rome and the collapse of empire set off reverberations in the late twentieth-century mind which were undreamed of a hundred or even fifty years ago.

During periods of apparent social dissolution the traditionalists, the true believers, the defenders of the status quo, turn to the past with an interest quite as obsessive as that of the radicals, the reformers, and the revolutionaries. What the true believers look for, and find, is proof that, once upon a time, things were as we should like them to be: the laws of economics worked; the streams of legal doctrine ran sweet and pure; order, tranquillity, and harmony governed our society.[3] Their message is: turn back and all will be well.

Until 1960 or thereabouts, American legal literature was ahistorical or even antihistorical. The treatises and the law review articles which date from our Age of Faith dealt with the historical development of the field of law under consideration with perfunctory disinterest. The writers devoted their considerable talents to the exposition of the present state of the law—which, by implicit and universal assumption, was also the final state, change having, by 1900, been abolished. After World War I, when it became obvious that the reports of the death of change had been exaggerated, the legal profession became obsessed with the need to keep up with the times. The annual pocket-part, which collects all the latest cases and statutory changes, became a standard feature of most treatises and practitioners' manuals. In the 1930s loose-leaf services were invented which kept their subscribers up-to-the-minute with monthly or weekly releases. Since the 1950s the computerization of all legal materials, with instant access to everything, has opened up nightmarish possibilities.[4]

In the law schools, until some time after World War II, the study of any field of law from a historical point of view was almost unheard of. Indeed, the Realists (with the exception of Karl Llewellyn) were no more interested in the past than the Langdellian formalists had been.[5] In the history of legal thought in this country few events are more interesting, or can have been more surprising to contemporary observers, than the explosion of interest in what has come to be called legal history.[6] Beginning in the late 1950s courses and seminars billed as "historical" appear, for the first time, in the law school catalogues. What is more, these offerings have been, and continue to be, largely subscribed by interested students. During the same twenty-year period the law reviews have published more historical material, written for the most part by the younger generation of academic lawyers, than had, I dare say, been published over the preceding hundred years. Indeed, specialized journals devoted exclusively to the publication of articles on legal history have made their appearance, and the academics who look on themselves as legal historians have organized in groups, sections, and associations. Since the foundations follow the fashions, there is even a good deal of money in the legal history game—an idea which, a generation ago, would have seemed fanciful.

I assume that the hold which legal history has currently acquired on the legal imagination is one reflection of the crisis of Western thought. In the writing of legal history, as in the writing of general history, both left-wing revisionists and right-wing traditionalists have been active. No doubt, the past is here to stay, but what the past really was becomes, each year, a little more obscure. The one thing that is clear is that no one, except speakers on ceremonial occasions, any longer believes the comforting eighteenth-century myth about the inevitability of progress.

III

The extraordinary achievement of our first half century of law may well have contributed to the excesses of the following half century. In the 1870s it must have been tempting to conclude that since, through law, much had been achieved, it followed that, through law, everything could be achieved, including the ultimate goals of scientific prediction and the control of the future course of our society. In the 1970s we look back on an unpleasant half century which has been largely devoted to destroying the illusions which had commended themselves to the men of the 1870s.

It is not surprising that, during this unpleasant period, the official legal establishment, in one of the great advertising campaigns of all time, sought to sell the integrity of the legal product, warranted to insure the salvation of our society. The idea of law was ridiculously oversold, which led to great confusion in the public mind when it became clear that ours is a government not of laws but of men and that justice under law is notably unequal.

May 1 of each year has been set aside as Law Day. On that day, speakers go forth from the bar associations to expound to the Rotary Clubs and the high schools the virtues of the Rule of Law in a Free Society. What is meant by the Rule of Law is rarely explained with any particularity, but the message is clear: we have the Rule of Law; our enemies do not have the Rule of Law; our possession of the Rule of Law is what makes our society a better society than their society.

The Rule of Law idea has also had its advocates on a less absurdly politicized level. In its respectable academic version the idea emphasizes principally the importance of procedural due process, the nice observance of established rules, the right of the accused to confront his accuser in open court before he is sent to jail.[7] Academics who promote the Rule of Law have also been, almost without exception, enthusiastic promoters of one or both of two ideas which enjoyed a great vogue during the 1950s. One was the idea which was summed up in the slogan: the End of Ideology. That meant that, in the United States as of 1950 or thereabouts, all the great social, political, and economic issues had been, for all time, satisfactorily solved. All that remained was to keep the great machine running smoothly—a maintenance job for technicians. The other idea also had its slogan: World Peace through World Law—an attractive proposition which enlisted the suffrage of many men of good will. World Peace through World Law seemed to mean that all disputes between nations not only should but could be settled by courts (or international organizations like courts) in the light of legal rules drawn up ahead of time. Implicit in the World Peace through World Law idea was the assumption that the territorial division and the distribution of power in the world, as it existed in the 1950s, was on the whole satisfactory and should not be changed.

The three slogans—the Rule of Law, the End of Ideology, World Peace through World Law—all assumed that the society we had achieved in the 1950s was a good one, that it must be preserved from attack by its enemies (who were usually identified as the Communist powers or, more broadly, the adherents of Marxist ideology), and that the function of law was to insure stability and guarantee us against change. The leading spokesmen for these ideas in the 1950s thought of themselves, and were thought of by others, as liberals in the great tradition. They were supporters of the New Deal reforms and many of them had held office under Roosevelt and Truman, as they later did under Kennedy and Johnson. The greatest difficulty in understanding what was going on in the United States through the 1950s is that ideological positions which now seem to have been conservative or reactionary were then seriously put forward as liberal, even radical.

The cheerfully meaningless slogans of the 1950s have not survived the national and international chaos of the 1960s and 1970s. The End of Ideology and World Peace through World Law already have a quaintly old-fashioned sound, and it is only an occasional unreconstructed cold warrior who still proclaims the virtues of the Rule of Law. But the conservative reaction which inspired the political slogans may, on a much more sophisticated level, still be with us.[8]

In 1970 I delivered a series of lectures which were later published under the catchy but misleading title, *The Death of Contract.* I ended the last of the lectures in this way:

> We have witnessed the dismantling of the formal system of the classical theorists. We have gone through our romantic agony—an experience peculiarly unsettling to people intellectually trained and conditioned as lawyers are. It may be that, in this centennial year, some new Langdell is already waiting in the wings to summon us back to the paths of righteousness, discipline, order, and well-articulated theory. Contract is dead— but who knows what unlikely resurrection the Eastertide may bring?[9]

In 1970 I thought of the passage I have quoted as merely a rhetorical flourish which, I hoped, might induce the audience to leave quietly without actually throwing things at me. I seem to have been a better prophet than I had dreamed of being. Our new Langdell may not yet have made his appearance on front-and-center stage but it is already apparent that the cause of well-articulated theory has been better served in the 1970s than, arguably, it has been in any decade since the 1870s. Forsaking the pluralism of such scholars as Corbin, Llewellyn, and Kessler,[10] the New Conceptualists, as they have been dubbed in some quarters, have returned to the elaboration of unitary theories, to the reduction of all principles of liability to Holmes's "philosophically continuous series."[11]

Their work is being taken seriously, as of course it should be. In the world of legal scholarship the New Conceptualism will be a force to be reckoned with for at least the next generation. It is, however, unlikely that its future includes a triumph as complete as that of Langdellianism a century ago. In the polarized society which we seem to have arrived at, consensus is an unlikely issue.

The vice of the formalistic approach to law, on the level of serious scholarship as on the level of political slogans and advertising campaigns, is that it leads to a disastrous overstatement of the necessary limits of law. In our own history, both in the late nineteenth century and in our own time, the components of the formalistic approach have included the search for theoretical formulas assumed to be of universal validity and the insistence that all particular instances should be analyzed and dealt with in the light of the overall theoretical structure. Solutions to problems are "right" if they conform to, "wrong" if they deviate from, that structure. The theoretical model itself quickly becomes frozen, so that what was "right" or "wrong" in 1870 must be equally "right" or "wrong" in 1920; what is "right" or "wrong" in 1970 will be equally so in the no doubt magical year of double twenty. The adept of formalism, once he has perfected his model (or borrowed one ready-made from an economist or a sociologist), becomes an advocate of stability and an enemy of further change. This process takes place quite as inexorably with respect to theories or models which were in their origins radical or revolutionary as it does with respect to those which in their origins were conservative or traditionalist. Thus during periods when the formalistic approach is dominant, the stare decisis idea inevitably comes to the fore along with the idea that the courts, without legislative sanction, are precluded from making any innovations on their own. Decision becomes a mechanistic process in which it is forbidden to look beyond the letter of the statute and the holding of the last case. The result, both in the legal mind and in the popular mind, is the deeply held belief that law is an engine for curbing our social ills through an enforced adherence to predetermined patterns of behavior.

I do not propose that we embrace chaos and all become anarchists as the only escape from the excesses of formalism. I do suggest that the lesson of the past two hundred years is that we will do well to be on our guard against all-purpose theoretical solutions to our problems. As lawyers we will do well to be on our guard against any suggestion that, through law, our society can be reformed, purified, or saved. The function of law, in a society like our own, is altogether more modest and less apocalyptic. It is to provide a mechanism for the settlement of disputes in the light of broadly conceived principles on whose soundness, it must be assumed, there is a general consensus among us. If the assumption is wrong, if there is no consensus, then we are headed for war, civil strife, and revolution, and the orderly administration of justice will become an irrelevant, nostalgic whimsy until the social fabric has been stitched together again and a new consensus has emerged. But, so long as the consensus exists, the mechanism which the law provides is designed to insure that our institutions adjust to change, which is inevitable, in a continuing process which will be orderly, gradual, and, to the extent that such a thing is possible in human affairs, rational. The function of the lawyer is to preserve a skeptical relativism in a society hell-bent for absolutes. When we become too sure of our premises, we necessarily fail in what we are supposed to be doing.

When we think of our own or of any other legal system, the beginning of wisdom lies in the recognition that the body

of the law, at any time or place, is an unstable mass in pre-
carious equilibrium. The study of our legal past is helpful to
lawyers and judges and legislators in the same way that the
study of recorded games is helpful to a chess player. But the
principal lesson to be drawn from our study is that the part
of wisdom is to keep our theories open-ended, our assumptions tentative, our reactions flexible. We must act, we must
decide, we must go this way or that. Like the blind men dealing with the elephant, we must erect hypotheses on the basis
of inadequate evidence. That does no harm—at all events it
is the human condition from which we will not escape—so
long as we do not delude ourselves into thinking that we have
finally seen our elephant whole.

IV

I shall conclude by paraphrasing Holmes.[12]

Law reflects but in no sense determines the moral worth
of a society. The values of a reasonably just society will reflect
themselves in a reasonably just law. The better the society, the
less law there will be. In Heaven there will be no law, and the
lion will lie down with the lamb. The values of an unjust society will reflect themselves in an unjust law. The worse the
society, the more law there will be. In Hell there will be nothing but law, and due process will be meticulously observed.

6

The Age of Consent

Philip Bobbitt

I

So what happened next? Did the society of which Gilmore wrote in the 1970s become more—or less—just, an assessment Gilmore claimed we could make by examining its laws?[1] There are encouraging signs that it did become more just, such as the broadening of access to health care by federal statute,[2] and the Supreme Court's declaration that the Defense of Marriage Act, which blatantly marginalized homosexual unions, was unconstitutional.[3] Or was there less justice, as the profusion of laws and regulations, like those of the federal tax code, was maniacally propagated, creating a jungle within which only the most well financed corporate predators could thrive?

I suppose the answer must be, as is so often the case with America, that all of these contradictory characterizations are true. We contain multitudes; we contradict ourselves. Law does reflect the moral worth of a society, and thus it is, at any time, a mass of conflicting moral claims and entitlements. But Gilmore overstated matters, as he knew, when he asserted that the law in no sense *determines* the moral stature of a society.[4] Because law guides and channels our moral intuitions—determining at what moments our consciences are engaged to resolve which questions—such assessments are necessarily dynamic and subject to constant change. It is this interaction between the static, studio portraits of a society as reflected in its laws, and the cinematic unribboning of law as it challenges, evolves, and shapes the very consciences that observe its development and on which it depends, that makes the moral evaluations of American society so complex, elusive, so *legal* in character.

Gilmore's conclusion was a paraphrase of Holmes, and it was to a biography of the great jurist and American superhero that Gilmore devoted his last years. The Harvard historian Mark De Wolfe Howe had begun the project, authorized by the Holmes Trust, but he had died having finished only the first forty years of Holmes's long life, before, that is, Holmes went on the Massachusetts bench and long before he was appointed to the U.S. Supreme Court at sixty-one.[5] Gilmore was not an unusual choice to succeed Howe. Though Holmes was known to the public as a great constitutional dissenter, his theories of contract had brought him early fame. Moreover, Gilmore was a thorough New Englander and a prominent second-generation Legal Realist; perhaps the trustees thought his reticent and fastidious irony would render Holmes as compelling to future generations as he had been to the early Realists. Gilmore shared with Holmes a rigorous skepticism about reform movements, partisan programs, and political ideologies, indeed about systems of any kind. What he lacked was Holmes's willingness to let the chips fall where they may, and it was this failure of detachment, a quality so essential for a Nietzschean figure of Holmes's martial temperament, that led to a paralyzing estrangement between the biographer and his subject. Gilmore died fifteen years after receiving the commission and submitted no manuscript.[6]

II

Gilmore's rueful writer's block reflected the conundrum into which Holmes and the Realists had led American law. Legal Realism posed this challenge: If law was simply what the judges did, then how could they ever be wrong—from a legal point of view? And if law was simply whatever the judges did—and they often contradicted and reversed each other and themselves—how could they ever be right? This unavoidably cast some doubt on the legitimacy of the judicial process.

This doubt particularly plagued constitutional law. It was one thing to say that great commercial and financial interests had influenced the drafting of the Uniform Commercial Code—that would hardly be surprising—or that the plaintiffs' bar had marshaled its political resources to effect ever broader statutory catchments for liability; that, too, was to be expected. But when the legitimacy of constitutional law was called into question, explosive charges were inserted beneath the very foundation of the rule of law: the idea that the state was under law. Most acutely, the American practice of judicial review was called into question, for if there was no reason to believe that the judges had a legal basis for their decisions, then why should we not defer to the Congress and the state legislatures or the Executive, who could at least claim the endorsement of the electorate?[7] If judges could never be wrong, then law itself was indeterminate—there was a correct argument for any conclusion—and the only explanation for the different results that judges reached had to lie outside the law in politics, ideology, personality, bias, and countless other factors, none of which provided, and many of which forfeited, the legitimacy of legal decisionmaking.

Gilmore's contemporaries working in constitutional law struggled, often heroically, with this problem. At the Harvard and Columbia Law Schools, Henry Hart and Herbert Wechsler proposed an answer. It wasn't *what* the judges decided but *how* they arrived at and applied their decisions that mattered. Judicial rule-applying must be a reasoned process of deriving rules from general principles of law—regardless of the substantive content of those principles—following those rules resolutely in resolving actual controversies between adverse parties without regard to their status or to any fact not explicitly made relevant by the rule itself.[8]

On the U.S. Supreme Court, Justice Hugo Black proposed a different answer: not the legal process, as Hart and Wechsler's approach came to be known, but the plain words of the constitutional text provided the bases for judicial decisions.[9] The Constitution's majestic absolutes—"Congress shall make no law . . . abridging the freedom of speech or of the press"; "Nor shall any state deprive any person of life, liberty or property without due process or law"—supervened and cordoned off vast areas of judicial decisionmaking where politics and personality were forbidden to trespass. These provisions were to be applied according to the common understanding of the words to our contemporary publics, and not reconceived by doctrine or recondite, legalistic constructions. "No" means "No."

At the Yale Law School, Charles Black—Gilmore's colleague and friend, the best man at his wedding—proposed yet another route out of the wilderness. Courts, Professor Black wrote, should look to the political structures ordained by the Constitution. American constitutional law could not be confined to constructions based on the history and text of the Constitution alone because many of its most important commitments lay in the relationships among these structures. The democratic process, which authorized judicial oversight, and not the legal process isolated in an apolitical vacuum, legitimated legal rulemaking, for example. This could be inferred from the relationship between Article I and Article III of the Constitution whereby Congress established the federal court system, endowed it with jurisdiction, and expected it to apply the statutes the Congress had passed, subject only to the constitutional restraints to which the Congress itself was subject.[10]

Gilmore himself was intrigued by an approach proffered by the eccentric but hugely forceful Chicago Law School professor William Crosskey, who gave a new, post-Realist twist to the originalist position—the position that constitutional interpretation is a matter of recovering the original intentions of the ratifiers of the text to be construed. Courts, Crosskey argued, should determine such intentions by examining the language of the society from which those ratifiers came.[11] Teasing out meaning from history had often been cited by Realists as leading to labyrinths of indeterminacy, but Crosskey claimed we could avoid such mazes by taking words and phrases on their own historical terms and building up meaning to arrive at original intentions rather than the other way around,[12] as originalists had customarily done.

Alexander Bickel, a colleague of Gilmore's and Black's at Yale, pressed yet another alternative. Extending an approach with origins in the jurisprudence of Louis Brandeis and Felix Frankfurter, Bickel argued that the practical consequences for the institutions of the law should guide judges in deciding how (or even whether) to apply the provisions and precedents of the Constitution.[13] As with the other, second-generation Realist approaches, Bickel's sought a calculus long ratified by common law—in his case, a comparison of the costs and benefits of a proposed rule—and tried to connect it to a fixed position mandated by the Constitution, the institutional position of the judiciary, thereby limiting the discretion of judges and protecting their stature.

Finally an outsider—if a philosophy professor educated at Princeton and teaching at Harvard can be deemed so—claimed that legitimacy for the rules of government could be established by applying a simple test. What rule, John Rawls asked, would we all agree to in the absence of any knowledge about its impact on ourselves?[14] Such a rule derives from the guiding ethos of any society whose laws are indifferent to the political, social, and economic interests of those who wield power—even the power of a majority of the electorate. Law professors—most influentially Ronald Dworkin—judges, and advocates, some who hadn't read the philosopher or perhaps did not even know his name, adopted this approach or others derived from it,[15] in the hope of finding that moral principle, that saving, generative ethical theory, that would allow them to decline the wormwood chalice proffered by Legal Realism.

Each approach enjoyed a temporary preeminence—even Crosskey's unusual historicism, which has recently experienced a renaissance[16]—but ultimately no one approach was able wholly to succeed because none was able to capture the unreflective consensus enjoyed by Formalism in its Age of Faith. New alignments formed, composed of the various approaches that had failed to achieve a stable hegemony: "strict construction"—composed of historical, textual, and structural elements—vied with a congeries of allegedly more latitudinarian forms—doctrinal, prudential, and ethical methods of interpretation—that its opponents ingenuously decried as "judicial activism." But this simplifying, contrapuntal division made the problem posed by Legal Realism harder, because there was no legal reason to prefer one set of approaches to another beyond the claim that each made that it alone was lawful, on its terms. Gilmore's Age of Anxiety had become an age of uncertainty, of ambiguity, of incompleteness. Despite Llewellyn's hopes for a renewal of the Grand Style of judging, instead we witnessed a new and barbaric Formal Style, as Gilmore bitterly foresaw. Indeed the whole history of American law might have been summed up in Zbigniew Herbert's short poem "From Mythology":

> First there was a god of night and tempest, a black idol without eyes, before whom they leaped, naked and smeared with blood. Later on, in the times of the republic, there were many gods with wives, children, creaking beds, and harmlessly exploding thunderbolts. At the end only superstitious neurotics carried in their pockets little statues of salt, representing the god of irony. There was no greater god at that time.
>
> Then came the barbarians. They too valued highly the little god of irony. They would crush it under their heels and add it to their dishes.[17]

The attitude of the vandals was simply put by a constitutional lawyer, Martin Garbus, who wrote in the *New York Times* that

> [L]aw is just politics by a different name, and that most Supreme Court justices are result-oriented and choose legal theories (originalism, judicial activism and the like) as window dressing while they get where they want to go.
>
> Although these illusory labels can be treated as serious methodologies and may be of interest to law professors . . . the American legal system [is] . . . just another part of the government, neither higher nor lower than the other two branches, and one that must be muscled.[18]

This is a crude but powerful prudentialism. Unlike the prudentialism of Brandeis, Frankfurter, and Bickel it is not concerned with protecting and preserving the institutions of
governing—they are all the same anyway, on this view. These
radical prudentialists—Gilmore disparagingly called them
the New Conceptualists[19]—had forgotten, if they ever knew
it, the insight that "to realize the relative validity of one's
convictions and yet stand for them unflinchingly, is what
distinguishes a civilized man."[20] Instead, they hungered for
certainty. Some, not finding it after the exposés of Legal Realism, marched into a politicized realm of cynicism, clothed in
an idealistic truculence; others, also not finding the certainty
of science, decided to invent it. Two movements, Critical Legal Studies and Law and Economics, arose, the illegitimate
children of Legal Realism. They did not wish to slay their
father so much as inherit his mantle. These movements were
not uncultured or unsophisticated. On the contrary, their
leaders were among the most cultivated and widely read of
the legal professoriat, though they could often be uncivil and
in their need for a reductionist certainty could appear to be
bullying and naïve.

III

Law and Economics at first appeared to be no more than one
more iteration—if the most powerful—of the "Law and ___"
phenomenon that arose as a consequence of Legal Realism's
claim that law was a *social* science if not quite the physical
science envisioned by Langdell. Some law professors, like
Eugene Rostow and Guido Calabresi, also had advanced
training in economics. Soon, anthropologists, sociologists,
behavioral psychologists, even psychiatrists, many without
law degrees, began to appear on law faculties. Calabresi's *The*

Costs of Accidents quickly became a classic text, and excerpts appeared in the leading torts casebooks,[21] but Calabresi was clearly a law professor with formidable economic skills, not a neoclassical economist. As he himself wrote,

> The classical economist will show *ad nauseam* that those who were made better off by moving to a free market choice system based on full costs could more than compensate those who were made worse off. The problem is that such hypothetical compensation rarely comes about. It may be too expensive; it may be made feasible only through the levying of taxes that misallocate resources grievously; or it may be politically impossible to accomplish. In all such cases, the theoretical desirability of the totally free market approach has little significance in practice.[22]

But the Law and Economics movement was not simply the "Law and Alfred Marshall Show." For one thing, it was a *movement*. Financed by corporations and foundations, it sponsored a series of annual workshops for law professors— Arthur Leff ridiculed these as "Pareto-in-the-Pines"[23]—to educate them in the new skills of microeconomics and indoctrinate them in the manner of political summer camps. At its core, Law and Economics relied on two controversial assumptions about the world. The efficient markets hypothesis (1) holds that markets provide and asset prices fully reflect all relevant information and thus provide accurate signals for the allocation of resources.[24] This idea is an inference from another notion, the rational expectations hypothesis (2), which states a postulate about the conduct of individual economic actors.[25] It holds that these actors form and update their judgments in response to available information in an optimal way (rather than, say, supposing that the future will resemble the past, as in adaptive expectations). It is consistent with rational expectations that outcomes depart unpredictably from expectations, as even a person acting rationally need not have perfect or complete information. But it is not consistent with the postulate for outcomes to depart predictably from expectations, as that departure would make the expectations not rational.

Both these hypotheses depend upon a more general assumption that people behave in ways that maximize those outcomes considered by them to be most desirable, and that they know how to do this by acting rationally. These hypotheses are essential elements in the "random walk"[26] or "efficient markets"[27] theory of the pricing of stocks and bonds, the account of the dynamics of hyperinflation,[28] the "permanent income"[29] and "life-cycle"[30] theories of consumption, and many other applications.

They also promised to serve as the basis for a radical reductionism when applied to law. Legal rules—such as those that govern liability for breach of contract or the commission of a tort, rules that determine property rights or responsibility for crimes and the sanctions we enforce against criminals—could be evaluated and so adjusted that the persons subject to those rules would produce, as efficiently as possible, the outcomes desired by society. All that was lacking was a principle, which would overcome the political objections to exalting the efficiency of public policy over other values by explaining that the distributive consequences of such an approach were negligible, and a clever rhetorician who would show not only how this was done but, in the spirit of Holmes's *The Common Law*, that it had always been the implicit logic of common law judges, even if they were unaware of it at the time. Thus the cul-de-sac into which Legal Realism had led American law could be deftly redesigned as a happy, if confined, roundabout. If law was nothing more than what judges did, it "turned out" (a favorite, cloying phrase of social scientists) that what they did was microeconomics.

In 1906, the Italian economist Vilfredo Pareto provided one-half of the needed principle when he proposed to a society deeply riven by partisan and social conflict this modest intersection of interests: surely, he said, all would agree with a policy that made at least some people better off and made no one worse off?[31] The other half was given by the Chicago School economist Ronald Coase, whose famous "theorem" proved that when transaction costs were not a factor—when for example, information was equally and cheaply available to all market agents—liability rules did not influence the efficiency of the ultimate allocation of resources.[32] Whether the legal rule made the rancher liable when his cattle trampled the crops of his neighbor or left the farmer to suffer without redress, the outcome was the same from society's point of view: the two parties would bargain, arriving at the most efficient outcome—a fence, for example, whose cost was measured against the cost of the ruined crops and the profits of uninhibited grazing. The party who paid might be different, but the total cost was the same, and neither party was worse off than he would otherwise have been.[33] Taking these insights of Pareto and Coase together yielded this conclusion: a perfectly competitive market would result in distributions of wealth from which no one can be made better off without someone being made worse off. Any redistributive action— indeed any action at all to shift losses—could not make the market more efficient, and might well make it less so, regardless of its claims of justice.

Thus in the aftermath of the bitterly ideological conflicts of the twentieth century, an apparently objective method had been arrived at that eerily recapitulated Holmes's prescription.

> [W]hen we are dealing with that part of the law which aims more directly than any other at establishing standards of conduct, we should expect there more than elsewhere to find that the tests of liability are external, and independent of the degree of evil in the particular person's motives or intentions. . . . They assume that every man is as able as every other to behave as they command. If they fall on any one class harder than on another, it is on the weakest. For it is precisely, to those who are most likely to err by temperament, ignorance, or folly, that the threats of the law are the most dangerous.[34]

This "objective" method to many persons must have seemed right in the late twentieth century after the terrible wars to determine whether communism, fascism, or parliamentarianism would be the just constitutional order of the industrial nation-state,[35] conflicts that, by some estimates,[36] had cost 90 million lives, just as Holmes's formulation must have seemed right after a Civil War—in which both sides appealed to a just God—had cost the lives of more than 750,000 American soldiers alone.[37] After such suffering, the desire for a consensus independent of ideology became itself an intense, ideological objective. Now the Law and Economics movement lacked only a virtuoso, and it found him in Richard Posner.

Richard Posner entered Yale at sixteen and left four years later with an English degree, summa cum laude. He had a dazzling career at the Harvard Law School—first in his class, president of the Harvard Law Review—before clerking for

William Brennan, at the time the most liberal member of the Supreme Court, and then working as an assistant to Solicitor General Thurgood Marshall.[38] A red-diaper baby from Manhattan, he might have been expected to join the lists of leftist law professors at the great American schools.

Something happened, perhaps not so different in kind from the street violence that radicalized the German jurist and fascist Carl Schmitt in the 1920s. The turmoil on American campuses, from which some schools like Columbia and Berkeley have never quite recovered, seems to have led Posner to question the liberal—and liberal/legal—notion of reasoned consensus.

"Politics is about enmity," he once said in words that could have been written by Schmitt. "It's about getting together with your friends and knocking off your enemies. The basic fallacy of liberalism is the idea that if we can get together with reasonable people we can agree on everything. But you can't agree: strife is ineradicable, a fundamental part of nature, in storms and in human relations."[39]

But that didn't mean law was politics. Indeed it pushed Posner the other way, in a search for a point beyond enmity and sectarianism. This he found in Pareto and Coase. After a year at Stanford, Posner moved to the Chicago Law School, where he grew to embody its famous empiricist model to such a degree that now the school resembles him. His most influential work, *The Economic Analysis of the Law*, is now in its eighth edition.[40] It is a series of marvelous sleights of hand, reminiscent of the mathematical transformations by which identities are proved in trigonometry, in which each branch of the law is resolved into a species of microeconomics. These transformations resemble the just-so stories of sociobiology and neuroscience, and other reductive centrifugal methods by which all the elements not germane to the particular qualitative sediment sought are spun away, an art of which Posner is a master and of whose exaggerations and distortions he is quite aware. Indeed by overstating his case he has become the most-cited legal academic in the United States.[41]

Posner has many gifts, including a lucid pen and a refreshing hostility to cant, and these two are allied with perhaps his greatest talent, a Nietzschean detachment that doesn't "make allowances,"[42] a quality of anti-sentimentality he shares with Holmes.

Gilmore had identified, early on, the Holmesian legacy in the Law and Economics movement: "Holmes's strict definition of boundaries of liability, stress on the introduction of scientific and economic considerations to legal questions, and lack of social welfare consciousness have induced economists, and lawyer-economists, at the University of Chicago to claim Holmes as one of their own."[43]

But Gilmore also saw something more. When he gave his Storrs Lectures, his audience was shocked at the portrait of Holmes as the Mephistopheles to Langdell's befuddled Faust. Wasn't Langdell's attempt to found a "science" of law just the sort of naïve law-quarrying that Holmes and the Legal Realists had ridiculed? Wasn't it Langdell's illusions that Holmes, Brandeis, and Cardozo as well as Corbin and Llewellyn had sought to dispel? Yes, but not only that. Just as Voltaire and the *philosophes* had accepted the basic tenets of the ideology they professed to despise—and just as the Roman Catholic Church had deftly moved to assume the scope and power of the Roman Empire it superseded[44]—Gilmore saw a "community of interest" between the Realists and the Langdellians.[45]

Indeed, he went further. Though few appreciated it at the time, Gilmore not only saw Posner as Holmes's heir, but quite perceptively saw the Law and Economics movement as a repackaging of Langdellianism. In almost the last page of *The Ages of American Law*,[46] he quoted Posner's inaugural announcement of the *Journal of Legal Studies*, the house organ of the Law and Economics movement, with its uncanny repetition of Langdell's own goals, and even his metaphors:

> The aim of the *Journal* is to encourage the application of scientific methods to the study of the legal system. As biology is to living organisms, astronomy to the stars, or economics to the price system, so should legal studies be to the legal system: an endeavor to make precise, objective, and systematic observations of how the legal system operates in fact and to discover and explain the recurrent patterns in the observations—the "laws" of the system.[47]

Llewellyn had hoped that the reappearance of the Formal Style before World War I was simply an aberration and that the Grand Style would emerge triumphant.[48] Like Llewellyn, Gilmore saw in Corbin's pragmatic treatment of contracts[49] and Cardozo's seductive case-lawyering[50] evidence that a Grand Style was emerging once again in American law.[51] Indeed Llewellyn's and Gilmore's efforts with the Uniform Commercial Code's open drafting style and its vague rules followed by extensive exemplary notes seemed to confirm this trend. Constitutional theorists like Bruce Ackerman claimed to find in the New Deal reversals of Formal Style opinions a "constitutional moment" of such consequence that it paralleled the adoption of the Civil War amendments that announced the Age of Faith and the founding cases of the Republic that marked the Age of Discovery.[52]

Alas, reports of the death of Formalism were exaggerated, as the Law and Economics movement demonstrated.

Moreover, a simple indifference to craft, notoriously in *Roe* v. *Wade*[53] but no less in evidence in the jurisprudence of less controversial cases—whether striking at executive authority as in *United States* v. *Nixon*[54] or *Clinton* v. *Jones*,[55] or at legislative discretion as in *Reynolds* v. *Sims*,[56] or at congressional power as in *Garcia* v. *San Antonio Metropolitan Transit Authority*,[57] whether enforcing rights as in *New York Times Co.* v. *Sullivan*[58] or trampling on them as in *Bush* v. *Gore*[59]—such indifference is not sufficient to merit the accolades of a "Grand Style" even if it is heedless of the rigors of a Formal Style. Perhaps a lack of style fitted the age. Perhaps it was an age of carefree vandals who smashed up things and then retreated back into their vast carelessness and let others clean up the mess they had made. That suggestion leads us to the other post-Gilmore movement that, like Law and Economics, sought to build on the wreckage left by Legal Realism.

IV

The movement that came to be known as Critical Legal Studies (CLS) was obviously not going to be impressed with argumentative rigor by judges to whom it referred as "toadying jurists."[60] Far from seeking a way out of Legal Realism, CLS embraced its critique of legal reasoning with a passionate intensity. The Uniform Commerical Code that Llewellyn and Gilmore had crafted was too pluralistic, too craft oriented. If the Law and Economics movement tried to restore an objective, universal calculus out of fear of the unknown, CLS exploited this fear almost to sadistic depths, claiming that the lack of such a calculus meant that all was potentially permitted; what actually eventuated was the replication of oppressive hierarchies.

Two principles united the CLS movement: (1) traditional legal doctrines were incoherent, precisely because they were pluralistic; for every rule there was an opposite, equally plausible formulation, and thus the system of rules was infinitely manipulable, indeterminate, and subjective; (2) the system existed in this mystifying form in order to sustain a legal order that was the basis for corporate capitalism, distracting reformers and dictating who gets how much in society while legitimating an oppressive social order. Thus American law, which claimed to be to some degree autonomous from politics, was really only an extension of politics by other means.[61]

Although the CLS movement claimed continuity with the civil rights movement, this genealogy did not quite wash. The historic triumphs of the civil rights struggle were the *laws* they spawned, the Civil Rights Act of 1964,[62] the Voting Rights Act of 1965,[63] and the numerous and courageous decisions of the Fifth Circuit judges who fearlessly interpreted Supreme Court precedents to destroy de jure segregation.[64] The true paternity of CLS can be found in the anti-war protests where demonstrators had circumvented the ordinary processes of representation and elections, shouting down speakers, closing classrooms, and attempting to make the society ungovernable. That movement had not so much ended the war as forced the United States to abandon it; it was a heady experience that quite a few protestors were loath to leave behind. It created a generation infused with the confidence that the society looked to them for change and that they, rather than the elected and appointed leaders ostensibly in charge, knew how to deliver that change. In the universities, perhaps especially in the law schools, they looked at their older colleagues—men who had supported the war, often in melancholy resignation—and did not want to be like them.

According to its principal theorist, Roberto Unger, Critical Legal Studies was composed of three distinct perspectives: a claim of radical indeterminacy[65] that fed a deconstructionist critique, exposing the role of the status quo embedded in the assumptions of the American legal process; a functionalist, neo-Marxist position that appealed to the conventional left; and what Unger called a "micro-institutionalist" program that asserted that the alternatives to American practices had to be recovered from a canvass of the "institutional variations in present and past law" because such alternatives had, at the level of traditional ideological abstraction (e.g., socialism v. capitalism), evaporated.[66] This may have been news to Unger's companions at the outset of the movement in the 1970s,[67] but by the time of Unger's own Storrs Lectures in 1994,[68] the universal appeal of Karl Marx had considerably waned.

In the meantime, from roughly 1977 and the founding CLS Conference at Ann Arbor until today when CLS is generally regarded with disillusionment,[69] CLS ridiculed, insulted, and assaulted the liberal establishment that had overwhelmingly dominated the elite law schools. Duncan Kennedy, the charismatic face of CLS for most Harvard Law students, had grown up in Cambridge and had known Mark Howe, Louis Jaffe, and Ben Kaplan—all senior members of the Harvard Law School faculty who were widely revered and stood, like Gilmore, for a particular kind of post–Legal Realism that was "skeptical of any attempt at grand theory of either a descriptive or a normative kind."[70] They reminded Kennedy of the pre–Civil War Northern Democrats of whom Henry James wrote,

> Such was the bewildered sensation of that earlier and simpler generation . . . that . . . their illusions were rudely dispelled, and they saw the best of all possible

republics given over to fratricidal carnage. This affair had no place in their scheme, and nothing was left for them but to hang their heads and close their eyes.[71]

The Crits had captured something altogether true about the dominant post-Realist Law School: its members struggled to justify themselves when confronted by the very heirs whose patrimony they had attempted to preserve. Gilmore's generation had tried to rebuild a bulwark against Legal Realism; CLS wanted to make sure that didn't happen.

> A paramount issue was the question: what should the sequel to nineteenth-century legal science ("doctrinal formalism") be? The point was a contest over the method of reasoned elaboration: the purposive interpretation of law in the vocabulary of impersonal policy and principle. The mainstream schools of legal theory— philosophies of right and justice, law and economics, legal process—tried to ground this analytic practice at a moment when its assumptions were already ceasing to be credible. The point was to argue for another future for legal analysis.[72]

Some of its adherents—but by no means all—credit CLS with the success that the legitimacy of conventional American legal practices has never been reestablished. I would be inclined to attribute this to Legal Realism, but if the advocates of CLS simply mean that they renewed the insights of Legal Realism against those in Gilmore's era who tried to fashion a post-Realist jurisprudence, perhaps they are right in their claims. CLS was always redefining itself to avoid its critics rather than answer them; for example, to the charge that the movement had collapsed by the mid-1990s, Unger rejoined,

> Those of us who called it a movement did not intend to establish a permanent genre or school of thought but

rather to intervene in a particular moment, in a particular direction.[73]

Were there few constructive ideas? CLS was therapeutic, not constructive. The very suggestion that they should have a replacement for the conventional practices was a contemptible affront, an insidious effort to co-opt them into reforming an irremediable enterprise.[74] Were the leaders a bit too elitist, too upper-middle class, too interested in good restaurants, for the masses whose interests they claimed to champion? They weren't *Leninists,* for heaven's sake; rather, a new organized "left bourgeois intelligentsia" would one day merge with an unspecified mass movement to initiate "the radical transformation of American society."[75]

But to note these aspects of the movement misses its appeal to my generation. In the first place, CLS's leaders were considerably gifted at the doctrinal analysis that their predecessors thought so essential. As Daniel Markovits later observed,

> [E]ven as its practitioners deny that doctrine can decide cases, they retain a formalist's aesthetic love of doctrine (something lawyer-economists almost at once abandoned). If one looks at Unger's "The Critical Legal Studies Movement" [and, one might add, Duncan Kennedy's "Form and Substance in Private Law Adjudication"], one finds page after page of genuinely first-rate private law doctrinalism, just aimed in a direction almost exactly opposed to the one that traditional doctrinalists pursue.[76]

Moreover, its leaders had for many of my contemporaries a charm and rebellious attractiveness. Kennedy himself was an irresistible Pied Piper for some students (though an equally irresistible target for their professors). This was the advice he gave to students who regrettably went to large law firms:

> [Resistance] means engaging in indirect struggle to
> control the political tone of the office, say by refusing
> to laugh at jokes. Blank expressions where the oppres-
> sor expects a compliant smile can be the beginning of
> actual power.[77]

It is hard not to see why some linked such advice—as opposed to trying to persuade, by example, young lawyers to
abandon their customary milieu in favor of living with the
poor—to the prep school student, home on break, who tries
to shock his parents' friends at dinner.

While CLS built a large body of scholarly work that was
heavily freighted with inherited jargon—"fundamental con-
tradiction," "false consciousness," "counter-hegemonic consciousness," "ideological state apparatuses," even "deviation-
ist doctrine"—it needed the adroit elusiveness of its own Jack
Flash, a rhetorician with considerable terpsichorean skills. To
float like a butterfly escaped from the chrysalis of the leaden
law school, to sting like a bee—see Mark Tushnet's acid attack
on Laurence Tribe[78]—CLS had to have the dance step of a
Duncan Kennedy. Although convinced that the existing legal
and social arrangements should be free of the hegemonies
and hierarchies that currently prevailed—Kennedy proposed
that salaries for janitors and law professors be equalized,[79]
that students be admitted to the most prestigious law schools
by lottery[80]—they derived their influence in great measure
from their seizure of the commanding heights of tenured
professorships at the Harvard Law School, whose position at
the apex of legal education they gleefully exploited. Blocking
appointments on political grounds,[81] vituperatively attacking
colleagues in print, persuading the law reviews to accept sub-
missions they merrily called "trashing,"[82] CLS seemed, for a
time, where the future of law, or at least the study and analysis of law, lay.[83]

But CLS, while it offered a generation hope that a change of consciousness would open up as-yet-undetermined ways of avoiding the delicate balancing of values that the preceding generation had cultivated within the walled garden of its privileges and its power, was never able to deliver on its promise. How was consciousness changed by lawyers and judges if not by law? What did a change in consciousness amount to if its vision was not secured by laws? The fatal blows to the movement were delivered by other, more authentic movements—feminist and race theorists who had no trouble finding an Archimedean point on which to base their preferences and lever the society. CLS's most notable theorist, Roberto Unger, seeking just such a fixed point in the widening gyre, had ended his most famous work with the plaintive "Speak, God,"[84] but the feminists and race activists did not need any divine confirmation. Indeed what they sought was confirmation of their victories in the courts and legislatures; that is, they sought the very imprimatur that CLS was busily trying to discredit.

A young professor at the Yale Law School, Arthur Leff, answered Unger with a witty reply in the form of a "Memorandum from the Devil."[85] Leff, a commercial law scholar, had been plucked from obscurity by Gilmore and brought to New Haven. He saw clearly that neither Law and Economics nor CLS could validate itself in the post-Realist environment without privileging its own normative assumptions (whatever the merits, and these were disputed, of their descriptive projects). Without some external referent—without God's guidance—all our normative systems and intuitions were contestable, and if the contest was to be waged by legal argument, then the indeterminacy at its core that the Legal Realists had identified made the entire enterprise a bad joke. Of course the Crits saw this; that is why they claimed it didn't really matter that they had nothing constructive to replace the system they trashed. The difficulty they encountered was that while they were reassuring themselves on this point, the Law and Economics movement was putting judges on the bench, writing deregulation into statutes, and resolutely replacing the liberal state's hostility to the unregulated market with deference to markets untrammeled and undisturbed by law.[86] Things were changing all right, but not in the direction CLS had anticipated.

Leff skewered the Law and Economics movement for its counterintuitive pyrotechnics. Wherever Posner found an inefficiency, mocking the ineptitude of a rule, Leff simply asserted a different value being maximized,[87] and how could Posner say he was wrong if the ultimate test was what society actually does? Even if it was accepted that the common law could be explained as the result of unconscious, perhaps genetically driven impulses to efficiency—a bizarre marriage of Richard Dawkins and Ayn Rand, a union one would not want to visualize—this did not provide the basis to find an ultimate warrant for efficiency as the touchstone for justice (though Posner once claimed that justice simply *was* efficiency[88]). As CLS had shown in the discrediting of the liberal state, a mere practice could not provide justification for itself. The problem with the Law and Economics movement was that it wasn't conservative enough. It had nothing to say about the values of decency, modesty of ambition, deference to tradition, reverence for sacrifice, privacy, loyalty, courage, fidelity, or even simple honesty. It might be possible to link these to efficient outcomes—and if anyone could do it, the artful Professor Posner was the person—but there hardly seemed any necessary link and there were many obvious counterexamples. The problem with CLS was that, for all its defiant poses, it wasn't radical enough. It began as a Marxist movement just when Marxist regimes were being dismantled, wall by wall, barbed wire and all, in revulsion by those very persons it claimed to serve who, "it turned out," preferred a liberal state. CLS then attempted to transform itself through dalliances with existentialism, decisionism, structuralism, and eventually postmodernism, chasing the avant garde and arriving only to find its new partner was already *passé*.[89] Building on the powerful insights of Legal Realism, CLS added little insight of its own. It was foreordained, perhaps by their common lineage to Legal Realism, that the movements would merge, and this happened in the person of Richard Posner himself, who became the last Crit, denouncing the pretensions of legal argument to form any structure of meaning beyond the service of power.[90]

Leff died at the age of forty-six in 1981; an austere eulogy[91] was written by Gilmore, who died the next year. Gilmore speculated on why Leff had devoted himself, in what were to be his last years, to writing a legal dictionary.[92] There are some obvious reasons. It might have made his family some money. It was an open-ended outlet for his wit and clarity.[93] But was it not also a bulwark against his despair? For what the debate after Legal Realism ignored were the *words*, the legal concepts and doctrines we employed, deployed, criticized, rejected, refashioned, that had a legitimacy all their own. This wasn't justification; perhaps we still needed God for that, but it would allow us to go on. It didn't require that we throw away the ladder by which we had emerged from feudalism.

"Law and ___" had implicitly disparaged such an enterprise, even while it paid it the false and sometimes smirking homage of claiming to "explain" it. Yet as one of the most incisive American literary critics once wrote,

> Some critics make a new work of art; some are psychologists; some mystics; some politicians and reformers;

a few philosophers and few literary critics altogether. It is possible to write about art from all these attitudes, but only the last two produce anything properly called criticism; criticism, that is, without a vitiating bias away from the subject in hand. The bastard kinds of criticism can have only a morphological and statistical relation to literature: as the chemistry of ivory to a game of chess.[94]

To suppose, however, that the Law and Economics and Critical Legal Studies movements would appreciate that the source of their enthusiasms was also the source of their ultimate sterility would be to ascribe to them a depth of self-reflection even greater than the insights they ascribed to themselves.

V

The hunger for a validating foundation for law made an equally great impact outside the academy in the efforts of Congress, the regulatory agencies, and the judiciary to reduce the discretion exercised by officials. As a prominent Realist judge, Charles Wyzanski, put it, "[C]hoosing among values is much too important a business for judges to do the choosing. That is something that citizens must keep for themselves."[95] If, as the Crits had argued, "who decides is everything and principle nothing but cosmetic,"[96] then reducing the scope for decision by officials, toadying or otherwise, was a vital step in assuring fairness. If, as the Law and Economics movement had claimed, all decisions could be reviewed by the application of a discretionless, even mathematical, analytical rule, then repeated layers of review would eliminate the idiosyncratic and arbitrary, refining decisionmaking to that which most closely hewed to the calculus of efficiency.[97] The importunate and acerbic guests from Legal Realism that demanded a foundation for law do not depart if their demands are not accommodated, yet the result of trying to satisfy them is to live with their desires rather than our needs.

And so it has proved. After all, if there was no warrant for the assertion of particular values by judges, this was certainly true for less exalted figures like teachers or police or doctors. Whereas Gilmore's generation had tried to rescue common law notions of reasonableness, duty, consent, and the like from the corrosive acid of Legal Realism that exposed their biased, unreflective, and often contradictory precedents, the next generation struggled to find a technology of decisionmaking that would eliminate or at least minimize these flaws.[98]

It was already apparent that deep trends were developing in American law that would move its orientation away from the interest of groups, with which it had been concerned since the Civil War—racial and ethnic groups, unions, political parties, sectarian organizations, the underprivileged, and the marginalized—to a greater focus on the individual. Initially this was manifested in a "rights revolution" wherein the interests of groups against the state were vindicated through individual lawsuits. But by the time of this writing, it was becoming clearer that something more fundamental was at work, something of which CLS and the Law and Economics movement themselves were mere epiphenomena.

No doubt the most controversial of the Supreme Court's decisions at the time of Gilmore's lectures was *Roe v. Wade*,[99] which upheld the right of women to terminate their pregnancies. Here the rhetoric of rights proved problematic, however, as a broad political reaction arose that asserted the rights of the unborn, a group at least as vulnerable and underrepresented as pregnant women. One way to resolve this tension was to shift the spotlight from groups to individual persons. Three years after the lectures, the Court overturned an important rights precedent that had held corporations liable for the disparate racial impact of their hiring policies; henceforth, actual discrimination against the individual plaintiff had to be proved.[100] By 1995, the Court was holding unconstitutional the common practice of minority "set asides"—a means of assuring that a certain percentage of contracts went to vendors from certain recognized racial or ethnic groups.[101]

Perhaps this trend to empower the individual began even earlier with the reversal of the right/privilege distinction. In an 1892 case brought by a Boston policeman who was fired for the expression of his political views, Holmes had written that the "petitioner may have a constitutional right to talk politics, but he has no constitutional right to be a policeman."[102] While courts had accepted claims based on an abuse of discretion by officials, the presumption lay in favor of the person exercising official responsibility. Now, widespread skepticism of, even hostility to, duly constituted authority replaced the deference of earlier generations as the public was persuaded that government officials had deceived them—especially regarding the Vietnam War—and were in collusion with powerful interests to preserve unsafe automobiles, pervasive pollution, and a rigged political system that favored incumbents and suppressed insurgents.

In the midst of the war, five high school students in Des Moines, Iowa, were suspended after they wore black armbands to class in protest. The Supreme Court announced that public schools should not be "enclaves of totalitarianism" and held the suspensions unconstitutional.[103] I doubt the Court realized that this decision protecting nonverbal forms of political action would lead, eventually and perhaps unavoidably, to the evisceration of campaign finance laws and the holding in *Citizens United* v. *FEC* that the Congress could not regulate private funding for political campaigns because campaign contributions—like other nonverbal demonstrations—were actions protected by the First Amendment's bar against laws abridging free speech.[104] For in a political environment dominated by expensive media campaigns, who can deny that once the limitation on the First Amendment to the spoken or written word is dispensed with, the checkbook of the millionaire speaks at least as formidably as the armband on an adolescent? If we weren't willing to trust the discretion of high-handed school administrators with an alleged taste for the "totalitarian," why would we trust the Congress, an ongoing class reunion of politicians, to set rules for the behavior of those who wished to unseat them?

A few years after the Des Moines case, four students attacked a school security officer after he intervened to halt a brawl in the lunchroom. The school principal, who herself had witnessed the incident, promptly suspended the four students. But the Supreme Court reversed the suspensions, holding that the status of being a student was a protected property right within the Fourteenth Amendment.[105] That same year, the Court held that students who had been suspended for spiking the punch at a school dance could sue school administrators for monetary damages for the violation of their Fourteenth Amendment rights to a hearing.[106] Subsequently, the Court extended similar rights to government employees who faced termination.[107]

One impact of what Henry Friendly called a "due process explosion"[108] was to invite protracted and costly jury trials—or the threats of jury trials—where institutions and governments had to justify their decisions. Increasingly these institutions sought to avoid making discretionary choices they feared might be costly to defend.

The fear of costly litigation infected many ordinary daily decisions. It wasn't simply that persons involved in the administration of schools, hospitals, churches, parks, and sports leagues suddenly faced frivolous and yet expensive lawsuits; it was that the consciousness of the ordinary person who had had little to do with lawyers now felt a threatening, litigious presence in the background of everyday life. It was often reported that a significant share of medical expense went to unnecessary, defensive tests,[109] and the popular press delighted in reporting absurd tort cases.[110]

Holdings protecting the Fifth Amendment rights of criminal defendants to remain silent and the Sixth Amendment right to counsel[111] were added to the Supreme Court's controversial exclusionary rule. The exclusionary rule held that evidence improperly collected—without a valid warrant, for example—could not be constitutionally introduced at trial.[112] Soon, criminal trials were chiefly about criminal procedures, which were in turn chiefly about the application of constitutional rules. This meant that guilty, often dangerous defendants were acquitted on what were obvious "technicalities," that is, flaws in the prosecution of the case that did not affect the guilt or innocence of the defendant. A prominent lawyer and public interest advocate, Philip Howard, concluded, "In the place of officials who had been unfair, [now there were] self-interested individuals [who] bullied the rest of society. . . . Race relations were strained, government unresponsive, schools unmanageable and [criminal] justice perceived as a game."[113]

Whatever the effects of these developments on institutional practices, the consequences for the standing of lawyers and the legal profession were catastrophic. While the number of lawyers doubled in the quarter century after Gilmore's lectures,[114] their standing in the public eye plum-

meted. In 1977, the Supreme Court handed down its decision in *Bates* v. *State Bar of Arizona*[115] striking down a ban
on advertising by lawyers. Holding that such advertising was
commercial speech protected by the First Amendment, the
Court reasoned that the public's access to information about
the pricing and availability of legal services outweighed the
bar's desire to maintain an image of professionalism. "Bankers and engineers advertise," Chief Justice Burger wrote, in
a remarkably obtuse observation, "and yet these professions
are not regarded as undignified."[116]

Just how far the public perception of such a change in the
role of lawyers went can be seen eight years later when the
Supreme Court handed down *Supreme Court of New Hampshire* v. *Piper* in 1985.[117] Kathryn Piper was a lawyer who lived
in Vermont but wanted to practice law in New Hampshire, as
she lived quite close to the state line. She submitted her application to the New Hampshire Bar Examiners, took the bar
exam, and passed but was then informed that she would have
to establish residence in New Hampshire before she could
be sworn in.[118] It had been assumed that, at least for the purposes of Article IV of the U.S. Constitution, states had considerable leeway in setting the requirements for the offices
of state, which were distinguished from mere businesses.[119]
Nevertheless the Court had little difficulty in identifying the
lawyer's role as essentially that of a market participant and
struck down the New Hampshire requirement of residency.[120]
The notion of the attorney as an "officer of the court" seemed
quaint.

It had long been an open secret that law firm partnerships
were becoming rarer and more tentative when they were
awarded. Partners didn't expect to stay with the same firm for
an entire career, and firms didn't commit to retaining partners in whom they lost confidence as generators of profits.

More adversarial relationships seemed to prevail among lawyers even outside the courtroom, depositions dissolved into efforts to intimidate and humiliate, and the Moloch-like rule of billable hours seemed to taint all participants who sacrificed, and were sacrificed, to it. Deborah Rhode, the director of the Stanford Center on the Legal Profession, described a deep dissatisfaction throughout the legal profession that, she concluded, was reflected in the high rates of stress, depression, and substance abuse reported in numerous surveys.[121]

From the protectors of litigant's rights, lawyers came to be seen as hectoring tormentors when these rights were no longer perceived as reasonably limited. But who was to say what was "reasonable"? Judges had been doing that—the "reasonable man" appears as often in judicial opinions as a butler in English country house mysteries—but something had changed. We no longer believed that the reasons judges gave for their rulings accurately reflected the true grounds for their decisions.

Partly this was the result of the late nineteenth- and early twentieth-century dethronement of the autonomous mind, a revolutionary defenestration as to which the Legal Realists had played the role of enthusiastic Jacobins. Minds, judicial or otherwise, were no more than brains, subject to the vagaries of billions of chance, evolutionary twists of the helical ascent by which man had abandoned his brother the chimpanzee; minds were "conditioned" by class preferences and the cultural hegemony of ruling groups; minds were unconscious, pushed by the lingering effects of unrecognized and distant traumas, pulled by the attractions of pheromones and artfully shaped chrome automobile grilles.

But mainly, the discrediting of judicial autonomy sprang from the same origin as the discrediting of the autonomy of law itself, the move from observing that law was no more than whatever the judge said it was to the demand that we find out just what *was* motivating judges, if it was not the reasons they gave for their rulings. Thus was the green apple of self-knowledge cultivated by the Legal Realists and consumed by the Republic. If the liberal state's balancing of interests was the death of Reason—as Duncan Kennedy liked to quote—the death, that is, of Formalism—then what demonic forces were alive and calling the shots?

VI

This inquiry led directly, even inescapably, to one of the most insidious habits loosed on the jurisprudential scene, partly by journalists and politicians but also partly by law faculty and practitioners. This is the practice, sometimes accompanied by a sneer, that always and only characterizes the truth or falsity of a legal conclusion as the equivalent of an analysis of the person asserting it.[122] Any notion that law was a matter of obligations and duties was dismissed on the grounds that its purpose was simply to validate the corporate system—both CLS and the Law and Economic Movements seem to agree on this.[123] Legal analysis was properly then a kind of diagnosis of the prejudices and biases of the analysand, typically a judge. This approach assumed, blithely, that the analyst was free of bias and, more damagingly, replaced the rationale offered by judges with the alleged discovery of their emotional, political, and cultural attitudes. Where once the Supreme Court reporter for the *New York Times* had refused his editors' demands to say which president, Republican or Democrat, had appointed an opinion's author and dissenters, it was now considered obligatory.[124]

This approach did, however, hold this promise: armed with the telemetry of a judge's psyche (or political background, which to the commentator was about the same), the analysts, whether historians or journalists or law professors, ought to be able to predict not only the outcome[125] but the rationale that served its purpose. But could they?

In 2008, the Israeli legal historian Assaf Likhovski undertook an extensive analysis of the methods used by the CLS historian Morton Horwitz to answer this question, "What factors influence judicial decisions?" After describing Horwitz's efforts and those he inspired, Likhovski concluded:

> Whether we use the broad-brush Horwitizian approach to the history of judicial decisions, such as the one applied in [Horwitz's early work or] the more nuanced, complex, thicker, and culturally sensitive methodology used by Horwitz in his later work; a biographical approach focusing on specific judges rather than on the development of specific doctrines; a micro-history of specific landmark cases; or even the "hard" quantitative methodology so favored by political scientists engaged in the study of judicial behavior, we will never really solve the mystery and reach the promised land of certain answers to what is, ultimately . . . [an] interpretative pursuit.[126]

Which is to say that at bottom, these debates were about meaning, not about politics, for Legal Realism had demonstrated that simply following rules of precedent did not yield consistent *and* comprehensive meaning. This disenchantment not only tore at Formalism, it set the terms of whatever was to succeed Formalism. There must be some external, objective, determinate way to choose which rule to follow. So thought Posner, but also Unger and also Leff.

Were they right? Judges seem to report a feeling of compulsion for most cases and, most of the time, agree across party lines.[127] In this past Supreme Court term, more than sixty percent of the cases were decided unanimously[128]—and these were cases of sufficient difficulty to have made their way through the appellate process. And yet it was child's play—or perhaps adult's play—to show that there were often alternatives. What was going on? How could we reconcile the self-conscious, subjective reports with the analysis of judicial behavior that did not fall into predictable political or socio-logical or psychological patterns?

Just suppose that Legal Realism and Formalism are two different reactions to American law that depend upon a shared expectation. That expectation is that a legal rule is ei-ther true or false depending on its relationship to a fact in the world. The Formalist asserts a legal rule is true when, for example, it corresponds to a fact such as those asserted by modern microeconomics, or reclaimed by a study of the orig-inal intentions of the Constitution's ratifiers, or commanded by the text of the Constitution. The Realist looks at law and, finding a mass of contradictory or potentially conflicting statements, concludes that a legal rule can have only an arbi-trary correctness. For the Legal Realist, the legal facts of the world to which the Formalist would adhere—sovereignty, or negligence, or consideration—are no more than conclu-sions that obtain whenever a court says they do. Insofar as legal rules purport to be about the world of facts, they are illusions.

These two temperamentally opposite reactions share the assumption that a legal rule is a proposition about the world and, perhaps for the law graduate about to take the bar exam, this is true. But is it true of a judge who is commanded to follow a legal rule? I would say that insofar as a legal rule is used to resolve and to provide a rationale for the resolution of a case, it is not a proposition about the world at all. Don't mix a decent Scotch with Coca-Cola, don't strike a woman, don't use racial or ethnic epithets, don't curse in front of a child, don't wear brown shoes to an evening dinner party, don't disengage the clutch while turning a corner—these are all rules for behavior, but they are not propositions. They are things that we—we who aim to be respected by our friends and taken seriously despite all evidence by our families, we who know better—would not be caught dead doing.[129] Some are trivial, some are essential, but all are contingent. "To demand more than this is perhaps a deep and incurable metaphysical need; but to allow it to determine one's practice is a symptom of an equally deep, and more dangerous, moral and political immaturity."[130] Perhaps the greatest contingency is the human conscience—reflecting in part and often unpredictably countless habits and cultural practices—but recognizing this should not make us any less faithful to our consciences.[131] Indeed recognizing the limitations of justification should not diminish by one iota the legitimating function of our practices, when these are structured by the rules of the game. After all, a roll of the dice will never abolish chance,[132] and card play can never repeal uncertainty.[133]

If this is right, then the way a judge reaches a decision is almost beside the point; rather it is the way she explains it that counts. After all, it is the rationale that will serve as the basis for future decisions, not the simply the outcome vis-à-vis the parties. A holding that was reached by secretly flipping a coin but is explained by a persuasive rationale is sufficient; a holding that is reached by conscientious and even agonized soul-searching but explained unpersuasively is not. What makes the rationale persuasive requires a bit of training and cultivated thought. To the layman, all legal opinions will appear to be an arbitrary series of choices. But to a judge working within well-defined conventions of legitimate argument, the application of a legal rule will often appear to be determined for her. This partly explains why constitutional law professors are badgered at cocktail parties by trusts and estates lawyers who deplore the lack of rules by which the Constitution is construed but take umbrage at any similar slight regarding the interpretation of the codicil to a will.

VII

At about the time CLS and the Law and Economics movements were gaining prominence in the legal academy with their sustained assaults on what Unger called the methodological consensus in law schools,[134] another approach— more radical in its way than either movement—made its initial appearance in constitutional law. While those movements sought to discover new truths about the law, this approach attempted to gain a clearer view of what we already implicitly knew about it. While they depended upon attaining new perspectives free of the confines of law itself, this approach depended upon achieving a more perspicuous account of the structure of our arguments, the medium by which we actually do law.

This approach studied the "methodological consensus" not to de-legitimate it, but to determine how legitimacy was maintained, as it was generally felt that legitimacy was precisely what that methodology lacked. As Henry Hart had confessed, the "legal process" does not provide any justificatory underpinnings; it may be a "thrilling tradition," to some at any rate, but like other traditions it can be employed on behalf of unjustifiable ends.

With respect to constitutional law, this approach focused on the claim that "all legitimate constitutional argument took the form of one of six 'modalities'[135]: appeals to the text, to

structure, to history, to precedent, to prudence (or consequences) and to national ethos."[136]

Sometimes called a "modal" approach, part of its usefulness
was that it laid bare the self-replicating set of practices that
were the basis for U.S. constitutional argument. As Gilmore
noted in his "Age of Discovery," the Americans took on more
or less wholesale the means of analysis used by the English
common law. What he did not say, and which is at least as important, is that these means were then applied by the United
States to the law of the state; that is, when the state was put
under law by means of a written constitution, the methods
for construing that constitution were those hitherto used to
construe wills and deeds, writs and judicial opinions.

Moreover, this approach also allowed different scholars
and jurists "to define themselves (and, equally importantly,
to define others) in terms of their favored modalities of argument. . . . Thus [these] modalities not only characterized
different forms of argument, they also characterized different
forms of scholars and different forms of scholarship."[137] The
law journals began to publish articles wholly devoted to the
nature of originalism, or textualism, and so forth; rich and
insightful books began to appear on these subjects.[138] Thus
this approach proved to be a clarifying way of analyzing any
constitutional issue from a legal point of view. This perspi-
cuity, this clarity, brought new light to some long-standing
controversies.[139] Of greater importance, however, was the
claim that such an approach empowered persons other than
judges. This was helpful for those questions, some of which
are discussed below, that were important constitutionally but
were not justiciable. Instead of wringing our hands because
there was no case on point or, worse, drawing the conclusion
that there were as a consequence simply lawless zones where
the Constitution did not apply—"the standards for impeach-

ment are whatever the House thinks they are" is one deplorable example—we now had at hand methods to resolve constitutional questions in the absence of judicial opinions. Indeed, "many social movements have reformed our institutions by daring to interpret the Constitution for themselves and by persuading others that their constitutional vision was the correct one."[140]

Yet in a legal world of differing and sometimes conflicting modal answers, how were we to resolve such conflicts? Which forms of argument trumped others? And if conscientiously following the modal forms assured legitimacy, what claim did this practice make for justice?

My own answer is that there is no hierarchy of modal forms, but rather than this being a cause for despair, it opens up a space in constitutional decisionmaking for the role of the individual conscience. The justice of the American system is not that it corresponds, or can be made to correspond by main force, to an external notion of "the just," whether Platonic or Marxist or what-have-you, but rather that it compels a recourse to conscience, which of course may be informed by our religious or philosophical or political convictions. It is true that constitutional theorists have, over the years, tried to create a system of constitutional interpretation that maximizes legitimacy by minimizing discretion; and it is also true that the modal approach, which has such promise, has not, I regret to say, deterred them.[141]

VIII

One subject has entered the canon of American law in the past decade, a subject that Gilmore had not anticipated. This is the "strategic turn" in constitutional law,[142] which brought squadrons of mild-mannered law professors to the task of integrating the subjects of national security—defense policy, intelligence collection and analysis, diplomacy and strategy—into constitutional law and international law and even sought to integrate the jurisprudence of two disciplines, law and strategy.[143] When Gilmore gave his Storrs Lectures, the importance of national security as a fundamental driver of the evolution of law was quite generally neglected; marginal subjects such as "national security law" dealt with the statutory frameworks for regulating the intelligence and defense agencies, or at most, civil liberties litigation that attempted to frustrate executive authority. Few in the 1970s would have suggested that the U.S. Constitution was principally the result of a widespread concern among the framers for the security of the American state. The preservation of slavery or the economic hegemony of the Founding Fathers were said with a knowing smile to be more probable causes of the movement toward a new constitution in the 1780s. Europe and its predatory empires were rarely mentioned as having anything to do with the founding of the American constitutional system. Nor did many law teachers treat international law as mainly driven by its interaction with war and conflict.

Perhaps the strategic turn was precipitated by the attacks on September 11, 2001; the sense of invulnerability Americans had hitherto enjoyed was breached (even if the actual threat was far less than that endured during the Cold War). I am inclined to think, however, that the intellectual foundation for this change had been building for a long time and that it arose in part from the experience of law professors and lawyers who served in national security posts within the U.S. government. On returning to private life or the academy, they found it obvious that just as law teaching had increasingly walked itself into a cul-de-sac, isolated from the prac-

tice of law, so had it wandered away from the real drivers of
state formation.

Not long before this strategic turn, I was approached by a
colleague of mine, a tax professor who had developed a keen
interest in the origins of the U.S. Constitution. "Do you know
why we have the Constitution we have instead of the Articles of Confederation?" he asked. "Yes, I think so," I replied.
"What do you think?" I said. "Taxes!" he answered. And I
said, "Yes, that's right. But what were the taxes for?" At the
time, no one focused on this answer, but the correct answer
was "War."

The strategic turn among the law professoriat was generally to the good. Constitutional law had become distorted,
driven in part by the due process explosion into an obsession
with constitutional litigation and criminal procedure, heedless of the source of constitutional law in the origins of the
state. Langdell also had a hand in this neglect. For while the
case method he introduced made a good deal of sense for the
study of contracts, property, and torts—common law subjects that were developed by judges—it made much less sense
with respect to constitutional law when most of the law was
not made by courts, or with respect to public international
law when little of significance had its final outcome in a court
case. Generations of students were taught that constitutional
law was principally a matter of judicial review because that
was where the cases were, and cases were what the Langdellian casebooks contained.

Such casebooks, collecting and editing appellate judicial
opinions, are not of much help for some of the most important constitutional questions. Among these questions are:
what are the standards for impeachment; can a state within
the Union secede; can the president obligate the United

States to pay a debt prior to the consent of Congress, as in the purchase of Louisiana from France; must the Executive seek a declaration of war before initiating hostilities or entering a belligerency; what are the standards for the consent to judicial or cabinet appointments; is the consent of the Senate necessary for the removal of a federal official confirmed by the Senate; and many others. None of these matters appeared in the casebooks of Gilmore's contemporaries, which contained long and intricate discussions as to whether the Kitty-Kat Club of South Bend, Indiana, could dispense with G-strings and pasties on its dancers and still retain the protection of the First Amendment.[144]

The outcome of the revolution in thinking about the security dimensions of constitutional law—a revolution that is still under way—has been largely salutary. Now students who are taught the Federalist Papers are not limited to No. 10, which was assigned little importance by the framers, nor are they instructed to skip the first, most important papers on war, diplomacy, and the need for a strong security state.[145] As to whether the legion of law professors who now fill the op-ed pages of our leading newspapers with their suggestions for Middle East peace, or the most efficacious approaches to Iran or China or Russia, have made lasting contributions, they at least did little harm, for the pieces were not taken seriously except possibly by their authors, and may even have done some good by engaging students in what is very much a growth industry in the law.

IX

One cannot speak of the "strategic turn" in constitutional law without noting the much more pervasive "empirical turn" that characterizes legal scholarship across the board.

Gilmore identified the arterial flow from Langdell to Posner: it pulsed with the idea that law is a science, if not identical to, at least similar to the physical sciences whose prestige was already mounting in Langdell's day. This simile gained plausibility in the case of Law and Economics because there was an additional step that brought greater verisimilitude: law was said to be a *social* science, and the social sciences were said to resemble the physical sciences. When this comparison also began to fray, yet another step fortuitously appeared. Law used—perhaps even required—the methods of the social sciences, and the empirical and statistical methods of the social sciences were like those of the physical sciences. As one scholar observed,

> The scientific method inherent in law and the social sciences offers a way of attempting to transcend mere personal values by providing empirically testable hypotheses.[146]

Leaving aside whether the findings of the social sciences are in fact reproducible and reversible like the findings of physics, it is indisputable that the attitude animating such a perspective has had an impact on the legal academy and its literature. Where once it was rare for those seeking jobs as law professors to have PhDs, now for the most competitive applicants it has become de rigueur, and these doctorates are overwhelmingly in the social sciences. This is not irrelevant, I surmise, to the fact that the articles in law reviews are increasingly "scholarly, professional, technocratic and less imaginative all at the same time [as well as] long and complicated."[147] Surprisingly to those who believe that the methodologies of the social sciences render their conclusions uniquely persuasive, the use of law review articles by lawyers and judges has plunged. About 43 percent of law review articles (to make a statistical point) have never been cited in another article or in a judicial decision.[148] It reminds one of the summary once given by Randall Jarrell of the criticism in the literary journals of his day. After observing that some of the best critics alive put most of their work in such magazines—Henry Monaghan comes to mind in the journals of today—Jarrell nevertheless concludes,

> But a great deal . . . is not only bad or mediocre, it is dull; and it is, often, an astonishingly graceless, joyless, humorless, long-winded, niggling, blinkered, methodical, self-important, cliché-ridden, prestige-obsessed, almost autonomous criticism.[149]

Such criticism, in trying to supplant the law with its own methodologies, seeks to move beyond the divisions and conflicts that are so endemic to the common law—of which our methods of constitutional interpretation are a descendant. If it be pressed that law is actually not a social science after all, such writers demand to know how we could ever critically evaluate law without making it the subject of scientific methodology. Surely the data set and the regression analysis will do what law has been unable to do: achieve an irresistible consensus. We don't *argue* about the speed of light or the molecular composition of water; why should we argue about whether law is doing what it is supposed to be doing, and how different rules would alter the way people behave in different circumstances?

The point of trying to assimilate law into the social sciences by appropriating their methodologies is to escape the mire of our conflicting personal values. In this desire, its advocates are not so very different from Pareto or Holmes. I confess I am skeptical that running away from the expression of our values will in fact achieve consensus, even on the rather minor issues as to which we believe we have the greatest statistical certainty. There is no statistic in law that is not value laden,[150] because it is introduced for a purpose and that purpose is to vindicate our values. That doesn't mean we can't agree on facts, nor does it mean that we can't find ways to go forward even when we disagree about values. That, after all, is what law does: it allows us to go on despite our differences.

X

I hope Gilmore's masterpiece of irony and wit stays in print to delight future generations of students. If this happens, someday a student will read these words as distant in time from their writing as the writer is distant from the evenings when he heard Gilmore deliver the lectures almost forty years ago. What will happen in the interim?

I diffidently venture two guesses.

This term (2012–2013), the U.S. Supreme Court handed down *Shelby County* v. *Holder*,[151] a case involving a challenge to the Voting Rights Act, which requires "preclearance" by the Department of Justice for redistricting plans in certain southern states.[152] Chief Justice Roberts, writing for the majority, observed that the factual assumptions on which the preclearance requirement was based—facts as to minority representation and voting in the states singled out—had dramatically changed since the adoption of the Act in 1965.[153] Because the determination that these states remained subject to the preclearance requirement was based on those now superseded facts, the Chief Justice concluded that the continued application of the oversight provision was unconstitutional.[154] There was simply no factual basis for departing from the constitutional principle that mandates the equal treatment of states. Putting aside the persuasiveness of this conclusion, it is not so very far from Gilmore—and Guido Calabresi, following Gilmore—who proposed that courts should exercise a common law function when dealing with statutes.[155] When the facts have fundamentally changed and when Congress has not been able to rewrite the statute whose factual basis has vanished, judges ought to simplify, cohere, even reject the ostensible commands of the law using the same methods of reasoned elaboration they have honed during the centuries of common law adjudication. If this does not happen, Gilmore and Calabresi argued, we shall all drown in the rising tide of defunct legislation that annually advances but rarely recedes.[156]

My second guess is no less radical, but I must unfortunately advance it without the imprimatur of my illustrious predecessors. The triumph of the years leading up to Gilmore's lecture was the "nationalization" of American constitutional law. Now, a burglar caught in the act in Louisiana is read the same rights as if he were in New York or California. Now, the requirement for a warrant as a precedent to a search by the police is the same in every jurisdiction. Now the standards for capital punishment, vain though they may be, are everywhere the same for the age of the person sentenced to die, his mental status, the crimes for which a capital penalty may be levied, even the methods that can be used. This was indeed a triumph, but it is not the end of history. We can already see the outlines of the next great constitutional transformation, as the American state evolves from one constitutional order, born in the Civil War, that attempts to manage market decisions—for what greater expropriation of private wealth has there ever been in this country than that accomplished by the Emancipation Proclamation[157] and the Thirteenth Amendment—to that of a state that attempts to use the market for the state's political goals, and even to adapt its methods to governing. Whether the subject is conscription, marriage, women's reproduction, or the deregulation of industrial practices, the United States is changing its basic orientation between the law and the market.[158]

This is one source of the increasing interest and impact of behavioral economics on law and other areas of public policy. Behavioral economists[159] had long observed that in assessing the statistical risks of various activities, the decisionmaker tended to be guided by an overall attitude toward the problem—an "affect heuristic"—that often skewed the appreciation of the situation. Sometimes people thought they were making decisions based on the facts, but were actually influenced by what other persons in their social networks believed—an "informational cascade" that led to mass movements that were otherwise inexplicable. "Framing" behavior often superimposed a general approach to a problem based on stereotypes and anecdotes that had little basis or relevance. Appreciating that much decisionmaking was intuitive, rapid, and emotional—rather than coolly calculating, deliberative, and logical—these economists, and the law professors[160] who were their enthusiastic followers, were able to suggest ways to counter these predictable biases and even to exploit them. If it was observed that persons tended to favor the path of least action—say in opting in or out of an organ donor program—and we wished to encourage donations, then it made sense to set the default action at opting in, requiring some particular act on the part of the decisionmaker to opt out. Or, at the very least, if we merely wished to enable people to make the decisions they thought they were making, and indicated when queried they wanted to make, there were various techniques to assist this by overcoming the known biases and irrationalities that were commonly observed. For example, if a patient wished to abstain from smoking or wanted to contribute to a retirement account, there were "pre-commitment strategies"—think of Odysseus lashing himself to the mast so as not to succumb to the sirens' song—that assisted in accomplishing this.[161]

Industrial nation-states, the exemplars of the constitutional order that arose in the second half of the nineteenth century and dominated the twentieth century, sought to tame the market by regulation, expropriation, intervention, and even direct participation through state corporations that ran telecommunications companies, national airlines, energy exploration and development, and much else. Now, that constitutional order is waning, as informational market states begin to emerge. Thus for example, we are moving from the state-owned enterprise to the sovereign wealth fund, as we go from trying to direct markets to using them to achieve our objectives.

This is quite different from the Law and Economics ideologies of Posner and his colleagues because it does not presume to set an overall political goal—efficiency—but either localizes political preferences in the individual so that the citizen stands in relation to the polity as a consumer stands in relation to the market, or assumes that there are some decisions that well-informed persons would always prefer.

Perhaps a more futuristic example will help to clarify the sort of techniques we can expect from an American market state. Consider the "nationalization" process I praised a few paragraphs above. We know from recent Supreme Court cases[162] that the government may not restrict the possession of firearms for self-defense beyond some very rudimentary bounds, such as prohibiting minors and felons from having guns. But suppose a person wished to live in a particular apartment house or even a "gated" community. It seems clear that the co-op board or the shareholders could make it a condition of residence that no ammunition or firearms be kept within the premises they govern. They might say: you have a Second Amendment right to have a gun, but you have no right to live in our buildings; if you wish to do so, you must abide by these non-discriminatory rules. This is an evasion of the Second Amendment by using the market, and I would not be surprised if many communities found it attractive.

XI

Of course, no one can really know the future because it moves away from us as we reach toward it—it does not become the present, as we sometimes assume. I, no more than Gilmore, and quite possibly a good deal less than he, can confidently anticipate the developments of another forty years. As we enter the Age of Consent—the era of a new, already emerging constitutional order that puts the maximization of individual choice at the pinnacle of public policy—it would be well to appreciate the structuring role for choice that American law has always provided. Far from obviating the need for our consciences, our laws structure a necessary role for them. That highly structured role is reflected in representative government (rather than plebiscites), in the composition of juries (rather than mobs, even when they form over the Internet rather than outside a jail), in the belief in liberal education (rather than indoctrination), in the responsibility of judges and lawyers to shape as well as defend the Constitution that gives them unique power. These structures will be strictly scrutinized in this era, as they should be. How else will these habits and practices find defenders unless they are convinced, after rigorous examination, that this way of structuring choice is worthy of defense?

For much of the twentieth century, however, these structures seemed to many quite tiresome, a series of barriers obstructing the way to fulfilling their desires most efficiently.

Why not simply insist on an all-embracing external ideology for American law and do away with all the contradictions and ambiguities that are so pervasive there? Yet ideology begets counterideology, and our body politic has as a result become more riven and divided. Instead of arguing for our values, a good many of our citizens have resorted to traducing those who disagreed with them, misrepresenting their views, even threatening their well-being so that all that is indecent, intolerant, and ignorant has steadily stained our public life, and many have turned inward in disgust and disillusion. It is little wonder then that, in the early twenty-first century, we find ourselves moving, apparently inexorably, toward the discrediting and perhaps even the dissolution of our constitutional structures. And to some this will seem inevitable because, after all, what could we do? Who are we to impose our values on others through law, when the market can so easily let every man be subject to his own values alone?

Great states do not lose influence and their ability to direct their own affairs because it is fated that they must fall. The lives of states do not progress from birth to certain death, as do the lives of men. Great societies lose their greatness when they lose confidence. For Americans that means the confidence that we can structure our fates through law, leaving the essential choices to the conscience of each person called upon to decide the question the law has posed.

Until God—or the Devil—answers our interrogatories, we must press on in the manifold ways our profession has taught us,[163] not expecting our questions to be answered definitively before a Final Judgment is rendered. The many efforts to superimpose a single, comprehensive ideological framework on the American system of law are actually inconsistent with the legitimacy of that system; its internal conflicts and contradictions are what provide the space for the role of conscience that is the authentic genius of American law.

This chapter began with the question, "What came next?" The answer to that question is the same as the answer to Grant Gilmore, who wondered at the end of his lectures whether American society would become more or less just.

It has been struggle, and perhaps neither gain nor loss.[164] For us, as for Gilmore, as for all those who submit their hopes to the discipline of an inherited but open-ended legal order, there is only the trying. The rest is not our business.[165]

> *Wherefore I perceive that there is nothing better than that a man should rejoice in his own works; for that is his portion: for who shall bring him to see what shall be after him?*[166]

Notes

1. The situation reminded me of the not wholly dissimilar case of Strunk and White. Will Strunk was a legendary English professor at Cornell University who, in 1919, privately published *The Elements of Style* for college students whose essay writing could benefit from some pruning of late nineteenth-century fussiness and overelaboration. One of Strunk's students was "Andy" White (apparently all red-headed students at Cornell in those times were called "Andy" after the founder), whose *New Yorker* pieces and children's books earned him immortality as E. B. White. Macmillan publishers commissioned White to revise the text for a 1959 edition (Strunk had died some years earlier), and the happy result perpetuated Strunk's devotion to "cleanliness, accuracy and brevity in the use of English." I held Gilmore in very high regard, as White had held Will Strunk, and I generally agreed with his ironic skepticism toward the various movements that, from time to time, mesmerized the American legal academy with their promises of salvation.

2. R. Cover, *Justice Accused,* at 200 (1975).

3. Id. at 229.

4. Indeed I mainly remember one particular lunch. After going back and forth for an hour, Gilmore patiently explaining why I should choose a more manageable research agenda, I wriggling loose, I had devoured another hamburger and Gilmore had drained his martini. He looked at me steadily, with his slightly crossed eyes through thick glasses, and said in his flinty, rock-ribbed accent, "Mr. Bobbitt, you are like the grasshopper [as Gilmore pronounced the word, it would have been rendered 'grawshop'pah']. You're *here,* you're *there,* but I cannot pin you *down.*" I realized this wasn't a compliment, and I slipped away from Morey's; Gilmore, perhaps in despair, stayed for a second martini. As I walked down York Street,

I passed the windows of J. Press, in which a tie caught my eye, a tie with grasshoppers. I still have it.

5. 84 *Yale L. J.* 1022–1044 (Apr. 1975).

6. The final paragraph of my book *Terror and Consent* concludes with an homage to Gilmore in the form of a reworking of the final paragraph of *The Ages of American Law.*

PREFACE

1. The concluding lecture in the series was published, substantially in the form in which it was delivered (with the addition of a few footnotes), in the *Yale Law Journal* under the title "The Age of Anxiety" (84 *Yale L. J.* 1022 (1975)). The material covered in that lecture now appears as Chapters 4 and 5.

CHAPTER 1

1. S.F.C. Milsom, *Historical Foundations of the Common Law* xi (1969).

2. The entries under the heading "jurisprudence" in the *New Oxford Dictionary* suggest that the first uses of the word to mean "philosophy of law" date from the nineteenth century. In earlier English usage the word had referred to legal systems generally or to their study.

3. There will, perhaps, be general agreement that economics and sociology were eighteenth-century inventions. My suggestion that history was another may seem, at first blush, surprising, since historical writing in the Western intellectual tradition goes back at least to the Greeks and Romans. What I have in mind, as the following discussion in the text indicates, is that, with Hegel and other writers, a radically different approach to the study of history manifested itself which emphasized not only a highly professionalized use of the source materials but a quest for the underlying "laws" of historical development. For a fascinating study of these changing attitudes, see M. Mandelbaum, *History, Man and Reason—a Study in Nineteenth-Century Thought* (1971). C. Becker, *The Heavenly*

City of the Eighteenth-Century Philosophers (1932) is still one of the most illuminating discussions of eighteenth-century thought.

4. William Blackstone (1723–1780) was the first holder of the Vinerian professorship of law at Oxford, to which he was appointed in 1758. His *Commentaries on the Laws of England* was first published between 1765 and 1769. It has been estimated that a thousand copies of the English edition were sold in this country (at £10 the set) before the first American edition (at £3 the set) was published in 1771–1772. Many other editions of the *Commentaries* appeared throughout the nineteenth century. See Lockmiller, *Sir William Blackstone*, 170–171 (1938). D. Boorstin, *The Mysterious Science of the Law* (1941) is an excellent study of Blackstone's ideas, which are for the most part incomprehensible to the twentieth-century mind.

5. William Murray, First Earl of Mansfield (1705–1793), was born in Scotland but made his career in England. He was educated at Oxford and was called to the bar in 1730. He held a number of political posts before becoming Chief Justice of the Court of King's Bench in 1756; he served in that capacity until 1788. His opinions are notable for their salty wit, their almost complete irreverence for the past, and their extraordinary sensitivity to the actual practices of the mercantile community. Mansfield established a "jury" of London merchants and was accustomed to seek their advice on mercantile custom and practice in commercial cases.

6. The case was Pillans and Rose v. Van Mierop and Hopkins, 3 Burr. 1663, 97 Eng. Rep. 1035 (K.B. 1765). A London banking house had agreed in writing to honor a draft to be drawn on it by a Rotterdam banking house for the account of an Irish client of the London house. Before the Rotterdam draft was presented, the Irish merchant had failed; the London bankers refused to pay. Held: the promise to honor the draft was binding; judgment for the Rotterdam bankers. Mansfield's use of the case as a vehicle to abolish the consideration doctrine is of particular interest in the light of the fact that the other justices on the court, who wrote concurring opinions, had no difficulty in finding, on one theory or another, a

"consideration" for the defendant's promise to honor the draft. The "strange and absurd" comment quoted in the text is from the concurring opinion of Justice Wilmot. Mansfield's colleagues on the court usually merely noted that they agreed with Lord Mansfield. The fact that they delivered elaborate concurring opinions in Pillans and Rose may suggest that they felt that, on this occasion, the Chief Justice had gone too far.

7. For the rejection of Mansfieldianism in England, see 8 W. Holdsworth, *A History of English Law* 34 *et seq.* (2d ed. 1937); 12 id. 595 *et seq.* (1938).

8. L. M. Friedman, *A History of American Law* (1973) contains, in Part I, a lively account of American law during the colonial period. Professor Friedman's interesting book, the bulk of which is devoted to the nineteenth-century story, appears to be the first attempt at a comprehensive survey of the development of American law.

9. See Friedman, note 8 *supra*, 282–285. A volume of Connecticut reports was published in 1789; a volume of Pennsylvania reports appeared the following year. Dallas, the editor of the Pennsylvania volume, became the first Reporter of the cases of the Supreme Court of the United States.

10. The practice of having only one opinion for the majority of a multi-judge court seems to have been instituted by Marshall when he became Chief Justice of the Supreme Court of the United States. Marshall's practice came under attack and, as late as the 1820s, proposals were made under which each of the Justices who sat on a case would have been required to file a separate opinion. See Roe and Osgood, United States Supreme Court: February Term 1824, 84 *Yale L. J.* 770, 772 (1975), citing C. Haines, *The Role of the Supreme Court in American Government and Politics* 512 *et seq.* (1944). The attacks failed and "the opinion of the court" became the standard practice in all American courts, state and federal. Indeed in some Western states, dissenting judges were not infrequently assigned to write the official opinion for the majority—an apparently nonsensical practice which actually makes a good deal of sense. If the

court is divided, it is the part of wisdom to make the opinion as narrow as possible, which a judge who disagrees with the majority can be counted on to do.

11. K. N. Llewellyn, *The Common Law Tradition: Deciding Appeals* (1960). Karl Nickerson Llewellyn (1893–1962) was one of the most interesting and original figures in twentieth-century American jurisprudence. A graduate of the Yale Law School, he practiced law briefly in New York City in the early 1920s and, from then until his death, served on the faculties of the Columbia and the University of Chicago Law Schools. In Chapter 4 *infra* I shall have a good deal to say about Llewellyn's work. On Llewellyn and his time, see W. Twining, *Karl Llewellyn and the Realist Movement* (1973), which I reviewed in 22 *Am. J. of Comparative Law* 812 (1974). I attempted to gave my own appreciation of Llewellyn in an obituary notice which appeared in 71 *Yale L.J.* 813 (1962).

Llewellyn's book, *The Common Law Tradition,* was the outgrowth of a series of Storrs lectures which he delivered at the Yale Law School in 1940. The original lectures were never published.

12. See, e.g., Horwitz, "Historical Foundations of Modern Contract Law," 87 *Harv. L. Rev.* 917 (1974); D. Kennedy, *The Rise and Fall of Classical Legal Thought (1850–1940)* (a forthcoming book by Professor Kennedy, who has graciously given permission to cite it). L. Friedman, note 8 *supra,* also seems to accept Llewellyn's periodization.

13. The post–World War I developments are discussed in Chapter 4 *infra.*

14. "I recognize without hesitation that judges do and must legislate but they can do so only interstitially; they are confined from molar to molecular motions. A common-law judge could not say I think the doctrine of consideration a bit of historical nonsense and shall not enforce it in my court." Southern Pacific Co. v. Jensen, 244 U.S. 205, 231 (1917) (dissenting opinion). On whether a "common-law judge" could abolish the doctrine of consideration, see Lord Mansfield's decision in Pillans and Rose v. Van Mierop and Hopkins (K. B. 1765), discussed *supra,* note 6 and accompanying text.

Of course, a great deal of water had gone over the dam between Lord Mansfield's day and Justice Holmes's day.

15. "The life of the law has not been logic; it has been experience. The felt necessities of the time, the prevalent moral and political theories, intuitions of public policy, avowed or unconscious, even the prejudices which judges share with their fellow-men, have had a good deal more to do than the syllogism in determining the rules by which men should be governed." *The Common Law* 5 (Howe ed. 1963)—a book which will be extensively discussed in Chapter 3 *infra*.

CHAPTER 2

1. See generally L. Friedman, *A History of American Law* 93 *et seq.*, 265 *et seq.* (1973). On the first American law schools, see R. Stevens, "Two Cheers for 1870: The American Law School," in *Law in American History* 405, 407 *et seq.* (eds. D. Fleming and B. Bailyn, 1971). The date "1870" in Professor Stevens's title refers to the reorganization of the Harvard Law School under Dean Langdell—an event which will be discussed in Chapter 3 *infra*.

2. On attitudes toward the civil law during the post-Revolutionary period, see Stein, "The Attraction of the Civil Law in Post-Revolutionary America," 52 *Va. L. Rev.* 403 (1966).

3. See W. W. Crosskey, *Politics and the Constitution in the History of the United States* (1953). Most constitutional law experts of the time, in a series of savage reviews, condemned Professor Crosskey to the ninth circle of hell. My own thought (speaking as a non-expert) is that Crosskey was in error on a great many peripheral details but may well have been right on his central argument. See my discussion of the attacks on Crosskey in "The Age of Antiquarius: On Legal History in a Time of Troubles," 39 *U. of Chi. L. Rev.* 475, 485 *et seq.* (1972). Crosskey's thought was that the intent of the framers had been subverted in the course of the growing controversy about slavery and that in particular James Madison had later falsified his notes on the Constitutional Convention (which were not published until 1840, after Madison's death). The two volumes

which Crosskey published in 1953 were designed as an introduction to a series of volumes. Because of ill health he was unable to continue the work. Thus the proof of Madison's falsifications (if indeed there was any proof) was never produced.

4. In Wheaton and Donaldson v. Peters and Grigg, 33 U.S. (8 Pet.) 591, 658 (1834) McLean, J., wrote for the Court: "It is clear, there can be no common law of the United States. The federal government is composed of twenty-four sovereign and independent states; each of which may have its local usages, customs and common law. There is no principle which pervades the union and has the authority of law, that is not embodied in the constitution or laws of the union. The common law could be made a part of our federal system only by legislative adoption.

"When therefore a common law right is asserted, we must look to the state in which the controversy originated."

The case was an action by Wheaton, who had been the Reporter of the Supreme Court's opinions from 1816 to 1827, against Peters, his successor in that office. Peters, on becoming Reporter, had issued an abbreviated edition of his predecessor's volumes (which had contained a great deal of commentary in addition to the opinions themselves). Peters's edition of the opinions for the Wheaton years sold for much less than Wheaton's Reports and effectually destroyed their market. Wheaton claimed that Peters had infringed his copyright. Judgment was for Peters. G. Dunne, *Justice Joseph Story and the Rise of the Supreme Court* (1970) has an interesting discussion of the case (at p. 323 *et seq.*).

5. Frontier attitudes toward law and lawyers are brilliantly examined in P. Miller, *The Life of the Mind in America (from the Revolution to the Civil War)* (1965). On lay judges and the situation in New York, see Friedman, note 1 *supra,* 109 *et seq.,* 122 *et seq.* W. E. Nelson, *Americanization of the Common Law: The Impact of Legal Change on Massachusetts Society, 1760–1830* (1975), is a remarkable study of many of the matters discussed in this section.

6. See Friedman, note 1 *supra,* 97. The word "English" does not appear in the statute as quoted by Professor Friedman but seems to be required by the overall sense.

7. On Lord Mansfield see Chapter 1, note 5 *supra* and the accompanying text. On the rejection in England of Mansfield's innovations after his death, see Chapter 1, note 7 *supra*.

8. See note 11 *infra* and the accompanying text.

9. I discussed the early codification movement in a paper delivered to a Conference on Comparative Commercial Law at McGill University in September 1968. See "Commercial Law in the United States: its Codification and Other Misadventures" in *Aspects of Comparative Commercial Law* (eds. J. Ziegel and W. Foster) 449 (1969).

10. Jeremy Bentham (1748–1831) savagely attacked Blackstone's idealized version of the common law in his *Fragment on Government*, first published anonymously in 1776. In his strenuous advocacy he seems to have idealized the virtues of a codified law quite as much as Blackstone idealized those of the common law. Bentham has become known as the father of utilitarianism, although many of his ideas have come to us as filtered through the Victorian minds of James and John Stuart Mill. J. Rawls's *A Theory of Justice* (1971) is a critical examination of the utilitarian premise which has provoked much controversy among philosophers and jurisprudentially inclined lawyers. At his death Bentham left a vast mass of manuscript which has never been (and may never be) published. One of Bentham's major works was first published in 1945 under the title *The Limits of Jurisprudence Defined*. Professor H. L. A. Hart of Oxford and his collaborators have been working on a new edition of Bentham which has resulted in the publication of *An Introduction to the Principles of Morals and Legislation* (eds. J. Burns and H. L. A. Hart 1970) and *Of Laws in General* (ed. H. L. A. Hart 1970). See also H. L. A. Hart, "Bentham and the Demystification of The Law," 36 *Mod. L. Rev.* 2 (1973). One of Professor Hart's theses is that the Mills, thought to be Bentham's disciples, had in fact distorted and diluted many of Bentham's ideas. A recent study of Bentham is C. Atkinson, *Jeremy Bentham: His Life and Work* (1969).

11. The name of Joseph Story (1779–1845) will frequently recur in the following discussion. The best account of Story's career is G. Dunne, *Justice Joseph Story and the Rise of the Supreme Court*

(1970), which I reviewed in 39 *U. of Chi. L. Rev.* 244 (1971). Appointed to the Supreme Court by President Madison in 1812, he served until his death. Beginning in 1831 he also served as Dane Professor of Law at Harvard and, in that capacity, produced a series of remarkable treatises (which will presently be discussed). His advocacy of a state-level codification as a means of avoiding the dangers referred to in the text was contained in an address on "The Progress of Jurisprudence" delivered to the Suffolk Bar Association, September 4, 1821, published in *The Miscellaneous Writings of Joseph Story* 198, 237 (1852). *The Miscellaneous Writings* were edited by Story's son, William Wetmore Story.

12. The reference in the text is to Story's 1837 "Report on the Codification of the Common Law," submitted to the Governor of Massachusetts on behalf of a commission which had been appointed to consider a codification of the law of the Commonwealth. The Massachusetts codification project was abandoned after Story declared that he would be unable to serve as draftsman of the projected code. His report for the commission is published in *The Miscellaneous Writings of Joseph Story* 698 (1852). The "mischievous . . . or futile" line appears at p. 712; the passage on "commercial contracts," which includes a list of the types of contracts he had in mind, is at pp. 730–731.

13. David Dudley Field (1805–1894) devoted himself throughout his long career to the cause of codification both nationally and internationally. In 1847 he was appointed to a commission charged with preparing a Code of Civil Procedure for New York. That Code, enacted in 1848, was thereafter substantially rewritten on several occasions. (See Friedman, *A History of American Law* 340 *et seq.* (1973).) In the 1850s Field became the guiding spirit of a commission charged with codifying the entire corpus of New York law, substantive as well as procedural. The five Codes, which were produced in an incredibly short period, were enacted by the New York legislature in 1878, but vetoed by the governor. That was the end of the New York codification movement but the Field Codes were adopted in the Dakota Territories in 1865 (the then governor was a close friend of Field) and in California (somewhat revised to meet

local conditions) in 1872. (David Field's younger brother Stephen, who later became a Justice of the Supreme Court of the United States, seems to have been responsible for the enactment of his brother's Codes in California, to which he had emigrated following the Gold Rush.) The California Codes were subsequently enacted in several other Western states. The California courts shortly adopted the principle that the Codes should be construed as having adopted the rules of the common law (whatever those rules might be or become); thus the provisions of the Codes appear to have had little or no effect on the development of California law. (On the subsequent history of the Field Codes in California, see Harrison, "The First Half-Century of the California Civil Code," 10 *Calif. L. Rev.* 185 (1922)). Opinions on the merits of Field's Codes have varied. Sir Frederick Pollock (who had been a draftsman himself) apparently despised them. See the *Holmes-Pollock Letters* (ed. M. Howe, 2d ed. 1961), Pollock's letters of July 18, 1918 ("the New York abortion") and May 11, 1927 (referring to the Western states which had "foolishly adopted" the Field Codes). What has most interested me in my own (fragmentary) study of the Codes (principally the Civil Code provisions on Contracts) has been the extent to which Field introduced civil law principles in what was supposed to be a common law codification. On Field see H. M. Field, *The Life of David Dudley Field* (1898).

14. James Kent (1763–1847) was appointed a justice of the New York Supreme Court in 1798, became chief justice in 1804 and chancellor of the Court of Chancery in 1814, holding that post until his retirement in 1823. The sixth edition of his *Commentaries,* which he had prepared, was published in 1848. The twelfth edition by Holmes, referred to in the text, contained elaborate analytical and critical notes by Holmes. Holmes himself had no great admiration for Kent. In a letter to John Norton Pomeroy (May 22, 1872) Holmes commented: "I . . . have to keep a civil tongue in my head while I am his [Kent's] valet—but his arrangement is chaotic—he has no general ideas except wrong ones and his treatment of special topics is often confused to the last degree." Quoted in M. Howe,

Justice Oliver Wendell Holmes—The Proving Years (1870–1882) 16 (1963).

15. On Story, see note 11 *supra*.

16. On the establishment of the National Reporter System, and its fateful consequences, see Chapter 3 *infra*, note 24 and the accompanying text.

17. The expansion of the admiralty jurisdiction during the pre-Civil War period is traced in outline in Chapter I of G. Gilmore and C. Black, *The Law of Admiralty* (2d ed. 1975). For a more detailed account see D. Robertson, *Admiralty and Federalism: History and Analysis of Problems of Federal-State Relations in the Maritime Law of the United States* (1970).

18. 41 U.S. (16 Pet.) 1 (1842). Justice Catron dissented on a minor point of negotiable instruments law but did not express disapproval of the main part of Story's majority opinion.

19. Which was to be held unconstitutional in Erie R. Co. v. Tompkins, 304 U.S. 64 (1938). The Erie case will be discussed in Chapter 4 *infra*, text following note 52.

20. 5 Johns. Ch. Rep. 54 (1821); aff'd 20 Johns. 637 (1822).

21. For example, Wheaton v. Peters, 33 U.S. (8 Pet.) 591 (1834), digested note 4 *supra*, in which Story had concurred with McLean's opinion for the Court. For the ambiguous and possibly discreditable role that Story may have played in the Wheaton case, see Dunne, note 11 *supra*, 323 *et seq.*

22. See note 3 *supra* and the accompanying text for the argument, advanced by Crosskey, that this had indeed been the original intent of the framers of the federal Constitution. However, nothing in Story's opinion suggests that any of the Justices thought that the Court in Swift was returning to a true faith which had been temporarily forgotten. Crosskey naturally approved of Swift v. Tyson (and deplored the Erie case, note 19 *supra*). See 2 Crosskey, *Politics and the Constitution in the History of the United States,* Chapters XXV, XXVI (1953). Crosskey rehearses the long series of cases (including Wheaton v. Peters) which Story could have cited (but did not cite) in Swift v. Tyson (which Crosskey discusses at p. 856 *et seq.*).

Crosskey's suggestion is that Story ignored the earlier cases in order to avoid embarrassment for the Court and perhaps in order to
avoid "unduly" prolonging his opinion (the latter suggestion being
less than persuasive, given the length of a typical opinion by Story).

23. See Carlisle v. Wishart, 11 Ohio 172 (1842), which involved
the same question (whether antecedent debt constituted value for
the purpose of cutting off defenses) decided in Swift v. Tyson. The
Ohio Court, overruling an earlier decision of its own, followed
Swift v. Tyson, commenting that "[I]n a country like ours, where so
much communication and interchange exists between the different
members of the confederacy, to preserve uniformity in the great
principles of commercial law, is of much interest to the mercantile
world." Quoted in 2 Crosskey, note 22 *supra,* at p. 856.

24. Examples, drawn from my own field, of controverted issues
for which the Supreme Court proposed solutions which promptly
became the law of the land both in federal and state courts would
include: (1) rights of bondholders under railroad and industrial
mortgages to property acquired after the execution of the mortgage
(Pennock v. Coe, 64 U.S. (23 How.) 117 (1859); United States v. New
Orleans R.R. 79 U.S. (12 Wall.) 362 (1870); see 2 G. Gilmore, *Security Interests in Personal Property* §28.1 (1965)); (2) right of buyer
of goods to reject because of trivial defects in seller's tender—the
so-called "perfect tender" rule (Norrington v. Wright, 115 U.S. 188
(1885); Filley v. Pope, 115 U.S. 213 (1885)); (3) right to bring action
for anticipatory breach of contract (i.e. repudiation before the time
scheduled for performance) (Roehm v. Horst, 178 U.S. 1 (1899).
In Robinson v. Elliott, 89 U.S. (22 Wall.) 513 (1874) the Court attempted, but failed, to solve a long-standing controversy about the
validity of so-called stock-in-trade mortgages under which the
mortgagor retained the right to sell the mortgaged goods (see discussion in 1 G. Gilmore, *op. cit. supra,* §2.5). In most of its late
nineteenth-century cases of this type, of which there were a great
many, the Court did not emphasize the fact that it was proposing
(or, in a term which has a current vogue, "fashioning") a "federal
rule"; indeed the typical opinion in such cases does not even cite
Swift v. Tyson. The Justice who is writing for the Court takes note

of the controversy which has arisen, reviews the arguments on both sides, cites authorities not only from state and federal courts in this country but from England and occasionally the civil law countries, and thus arrives at the Court's decision (which in nine cases out of ten was unanimous). The cases through this period, at least at the Supreme Court level, were entirely faithful to the spirit of Story's Swift v. Tyson opinion, which is described in the following paragraph of the text.

25. De Tocqueville (1805–1859) visited the United States in 1831 and 1832. The first volume of his *De la Démocratie en Amérique* was published in 1835; the second volume in 1840. The first English translation by Henry Reeve was published in three volumes between 1835 and 1840.

26. In the following discussion I have borrowed heavily from R. Cover, *Justice Accused: Antislavery and the Judicial Process* (1975). The idea that the moral pressures to which antislavery judges were subjected when they were required to decide slavery cases drove them to adopt the techniques of legal formalism is entirely Professor Cover's. He is not of course responsible for the use I have made of his idea.

27. As has recently been argued by R. Fogel and S. Engerman, *Time on the Cross* (1974) who purport to prove, with a wealth of statistical data, that in the United States in 1860 slave labor in the Southern states was more productive and more efficient than free labor in the Northern states.

28. Lemuel Shaw (1781–1861) served as chief justice of the Supreme Judicial Court of Massachusetts from 1830 to 1860. On Shaw see L. Levy, *The Law of the Commonwealth and Chief Justice Shaw* (1957).

29. See Story's opinion in Prigg v. Pennsylvania, 41 U.S. (16 Pet.) 539 (1842); Shaw's opinion in Thomas Sims's Case, 61 Mass. (7 Cush.) 285 (1851). In the Prigg case the defendant, an agent for a Maryland slave owner, had, without the aid of legal process, apprehended alleged fugitive slaves in Pennsylvania and returned them to Maryland. He was convicted in Pennsylvania for violation of the state kidnapping statute. In the Supreme Court of the United

States, the conviction was reversed (McLean, J., dissenting) on the
ground that the Pennsylvania statute was unconstitutional as applied to Prigg. Seven separate opinions were filed in the Supreme
Court (an unheard of performance for the time). Story's opinion,
which came to be considered the leading opinion, emphasized the
exclusivity of federal power under Article IV of the federal Constitution and the Fugitive Slave Act of 1793. Sims's case involved the
Fugitive Slave Act of 1850, which provided for the appointment of
federal commissioners empowered to order the return of alleged
fugitives (whose own testimony was not admissible in the proceedings), without appeal to the courts. Sims was apprehended as a fugitive in Boston and an application was made to Shaw, as chief justice of the Massachusetts Court, for a writ of habeas corpus. Shaw
refused to issue the writ, concluding in his opinion that the Act of
1850 was in all respects constitutional. Shaw was involved in several other fugitive slave proceedings, in all of which he consistently
maintained the power of the federal authorities, but Sims's case
was the only one in which he wrote an opinion. On the opinions
by Story and Shaw, see Cover, note 26 *supra*. Levy, note 28 *supra*,
Chapter 6, discusses Shaw's involvement in the Sims case and other
fugitive slave cases.

30. Cover, note 26 *supra,* after having reviewed the slavery opinions of the antislavery judges, turns in Part III of his book to what
he calls "the moral-formal dilemma." He comments (at p. 199):
"Whenever judges confronted the moral-formal dilemma they almost uniformly applied the legal rules. . . . Furthermore . . . these
judges accompanied their decisions with striking manifestations of
at least one of three related responsibility-mitigation mechanisms:
(1) Elevation of the formal stakes (sometimes combined with mini-
mization of the moral stakes). (2) Retreat to a mechanistic formalism. (3) Ascription of responsibility elsewhere."

31. That future will be the principal subject of the following
Chapter 3.

32. K. Llewellyn, *The Common Law Tradition: Deciding Appeals*
45, note 40 (1960): "Apart from our early nineteenth century, I have
come across the Grand Style only twice: in Cheyenne Indian law

and in the classical Roman period." Llewellyn's odd reference to Cheyenne Indian law is explained by the fact that, in collaboration with an anthropologist, he had spent several years studying the law of the Cheyennes. The resulting book, Llewellyn and Hoebel, *The Cheyenne Way* (1941) makes fascinating reading. Llewellyn's paeans of praise for the techniques which the Cheyennes (before their confinement to a reservation in the late nineteenth century) had developed for settling disputes between members of the tribe may well reflect a romantic attachment for their once free way of life. We will not further inquire into Cheyenne law.

CHAPTER 3

1. On Langdell (1826–1906) and his deanship (1870–1895), see Chapter VI ("The Langdell Era") of A. Sutherland, *The Law at Harvard* (1967). Professor Sutherland would not, of course, agree with my estimate of Langdell nor, presumably, with that of Professor Robert Stevens in his article cited Chapter 2 *supra,* note 1.

2. The quotation is from an address to the Harvard Law School Association in 1886, quoted by Sutherland, note 1 *supra,* at p. 175. For a contemporary echo of Dean Langdell's formulation, see Chapter 5 *infra,* note 11.

3. From the preface to Langdell's *Cases on Contracts* (1871), quoted by Sutherland, note 1 *supra,* at p. 174. Langdell's chief innovation in legal education was the introduction of the so-called case method of teaching in which the principal (in Langdell's original version, the only) materials presented to the student are the reports of decided cases, whose meaning is to be worked out by study and in classroom discussion. The case method, which was bitterly attacked for a generation after Langdell had introduced it, had, by the time of World War I, been adopted in almost all American law schools. Langdell's *Cases on Contracts* was the first casebook of all. Langdell's *Summary of the Law of Contracts* (which appeared as an appendix to the second edition of the casebook and was also published separately (1880)) is essentially a guide to the casebook, explaining which cases are "right" and which are "wrong." For more

on Langdell's version of the case method, see the text at and following note 11 *infra*.

4. On the early developments, see S.F.C. Milsom, *Historical Foundations of the Common Law* (1969). For a brief but perceptive account of the slow emergence of the contract idea from the twelfth century to the nineteenth, see the essay by Professor Kessler ("From Status to Contract") which appears as Chapter I of F. Kessler and G. Gilmore, *Contracts: Cases and Materials* (2d ed. 1970).

5. Powell, *Essay upon the Law of Contracts and Agreements* (Dublin, 1790), may have been the first.

6. W. W. Story, *Treatise on the Law of Contracts not under Seal* (1844); a revised and expanded edition appeared in 1847. The author, William Wetmore Story, was Justice Joseph Story's son.

7. The list in the text is taken from the "Advertisement" to the second edition of Story, note 6 *supra*.

8. I have given my own analysis of the late nineteenth-century general theory of contract in Chapters I and II of *The Death of Contract* (1974), a book which has not met with universal approval. On the critical reaction to the book, see Chapter 5 *infra*, note 9. Despite the book's many shortcomings, I have not been persuaded by my critics that my reconstruction was fundamentally in error.

9. Consider, for example, the title of an American book published in 1889, J. Bishop, *Commentaries on the Non-Contract Law and especially as to Common Affairs not of Contract or the Every-Day Rights and Torts*. The first American treatise to use the word in its title was Hilliard, *The Law of Torts, or Private Wrongs* (1859); the first English treatise on torts, Addison, *Wrongs and Their Remedies,* appeared in 1860. Bishop (at p. 2, note 1) quotes Sir Frederick Pollock as referring to "a meagre and unthinking digest of 'The Law of Actions on the Case for Torts and Wrongs,' published in 1720, remarkable chiefly for the depths of historical ignorance which it occasionally reveals." Bishop has an amusing footnote (at p. 2, note 2) on the refusal of American law book publishers in the 1850s even to consider a book on such an outlandish subject. He quotes himself as having remarked to a friend while they were watching a streetcleaner at

work: "Well, when I become too demented to swing a broom, I am going to set up in business as a great law publisher."

10. "Trespass" and "case" have already been identified, text following note 4 *supra*. "Conversion" means the wrongful taking or detention of another's property. The other terms are self-explanatory.

11. From the preface to Langdell's *Cases on Contracts* (1871), quoted by Sutherland, note 1 *supra*, at p. 174. On Langdell's introduction of the case method of teaching law, see note 3 *supra*.

12. For a few examples of the major surgery, drawn from the contract area, see *The Death of Contract*, note 8 *supra*, at p. 22 *et seq.*

13. Oliver Wendell Holmes, Jr. (1841–1935), who served on the Supreme Judicial Court of Massachusetts from 1883 to 1903 and on the Supreme Court of the United States from 1903 until his retirement in 1933, is the most celebrated figure in American jurisprudence. By far the best study of Holmes's early life and prejudicial career are the two volumes by the late Mark De Wolfe Howe, *The Shaping Years: 1841–1870* (1957); *The Proving Years: 1870–1882* (1963). Howe's second volume, *The Proving Years*, analyzes Holmes's 1881 book, *The Common Law*, which will presently be discussed in the text. Howe also wrote a perceptive introduction to *The Common Law* in his 1963 edition of that book. To avoid misunderstanding, I should add that I have, for some years, been engaged in preparing a book on Holmes's judicial career, which will be a sequel to the two Howe volumes. What I shall have to say about Holmes and his ideas in the following discussion derives from the work I have done on that book. I have analyzed Holmes's contribution to contract theory in *The Death of Contract* (1974), note 8 *supra*. Some reviewers seem to have taken—I would say, mistaken—my discussion as an attack on Holmes. It may be that some admirers of Holmes will take the following discussion in the same way. It is surely true that my Holmes has little in common with the Holmes of popular myth and legend. Holmes, to the extent that I can follow the dark outlines of his thought, seems to me to have been both a greater man and a more profound thinker than the mythical Holmes ever was.

14. A good place in which to observe the elaboration of the myth is the volumes of Herbert Croly's *New Republic*. Holmes, a great letter writer in his old age, carried on correspondences with both Laski and Frankfurter over many years. The Holmes-Laski correspondence (edited by Howe) was published as the *Holmes-Laski Letters: the Correspondence of Mr. Justice Holmes and Harold J. Laski, 1916-1935* (1953). The Holmes-Frankfurter correspondence has not been published.

15. *The Common Law* 38 (Howe ed. 1963).

16. *Id.* at p. 36.

17. On Peirce (1839-1914) see Young, "Charles Sanders Peirce" in *Studies in the Philosophy of Charles Sanders Peirce* (Weiner and Young eds. 1952); P. Weiss, Biography of Charles S. Peirce, 14 *Dict. of American Biography* 398 (1934), reprinted in *Perspectives on Peirce* 1 (R. Bernstein ed. 1965). On the parallelism between the ideas of Holmes and Peirce, see Note, "Holmes, Peirce and Legal Pragmatism," 84 *Yale L.J.* 1123 (1975) (by J. D. Miller).

18. For what Holmes thought of Kent, see Chapter 2 *supra*, note 14.

19. When the lectures were published, Holmes added a cryptic preface, less than a page long, which ends: "If, within the bounds which I have set myself, any one should feel inclined to reproach me for a want of greater detail, I can only quote the words of Lehuërou, 'Nous faisons une théorie et non un spicilège.'" Even buffs of nineteenth-century historiography may find themselves defeated by Lehuërou, just as those familiar with the French language may be baffled by "spicilège." Lehuërou, a Belgian historian who flourished in the first half of the nineteenth century, wrote, among other things, a history of the Merovingian Kings. "Spicilège" (L. spicilegium) originally referred to the remnants that can be gleaned from a field after the principal harvest has been completed. By analogical extension, it came to be used to refer to the publication of historical trivia after the main outlines of a period have become known. Perhaps Holmes threw in this mysterious, indeed almost incomprehensible quotation as a way of alerting the astute reader that what was to be taken seriously in the book was the theory, not the

historical details. I do not know from what work Holmes took the quotation. I am by no means the first to advance the proposition that *The Common Law* was a work of theoretical speculation, not of history. Mark De Wolfe Howe commented, in his introduction to his 1963 edition (at p. xx): "*The Common Law* is not primarily a work of legal history. It is an endeavor in philosophy—a speculative undertaking in which the author sought to find in the materials of legal history data which would support a new interpretation of the legal order."

20. *The Common Law* 32 (Howe ed. 1963).

21. At the beginning of the fourth lecture ("Fraud, Malice, and Intent—The Theory of Torts") Holmes briefly summarized what he had already said in his second lecture ("The Criminal Law") and continued: "It remains to be seen whether a similar reduction is possible on the civil side of the law, and whether thus fraudulent, malicious, intentional, and negligent wrongs can be brought into a philosophically continuous series." *The Common Law* 104 (Howe ed. 1963). The answer to Holmes's query was, as it hardly needs saying: Yes.

The discussion in the text draws on an unpublished paper by Charles Yablon, Esq., Yale Law School, Class of 1976.

22. *The Common Law* 76, 77 (Howe ed. 1963).

23. On the American law school, see R. Stevens, "Two Cheers for 1870," cited in Chapter 2 *supra,* note 1. On the Harvard Law School, see A. Sutherland, *The Law at Harvard* (1967).

24. As originally established (between 1879 and 1887) the Reporter System included the reports of all state courts of last resort as well as the reports of the Supreme Court of the United States and the reports of some but not all the cases decided by the inferior federal courts. Beginning in 1888 the coverage of the New York reports was extended to include cases decided in the lower courts of the state (a distinction which was also conferred on the California reports, but not until 1959).

25. See text at note 11 *supra.*

26. See K. Llewellyn, *The Common Law Tradition: Deciding Appeals* (1960); *cf.* Chapter 1, note 11 *supra* and the accompanying

text. L. Friedman, *A History of American Law* 334 (1973), seems to concur: "Many appellate opinions of the '80's and '90's are torture to read—bombastic, diffuse, labored, drearily logical, crammed with unnecessary citations."

27. See Chapter 2 *supra*, text at and following note 18.

28. The Supreme Court of the United States approved the practice of appointing receivers in Covington Drawbridge Co. v. Shephard, 62 U.S. (21 How.) 112 (1858) (tolls on a bridge); in Davis v. Gray, 83 U.S. (16 Wall.) 203, 220 (1872) Justice Swayne upheld the appointment of receivers for insolvent railroads "to operate such roads, until the difficulties are removed, or such arrangements are made that the roads can be sold with the least sacrifice of the interests of those concerned." On the history of the equity receivership, see 6 *Collier on Bankruptcy* §0.04 (14th ed., revised 1972).

29. On Erie R. Co. v. Tompkins, 304 U.S. 64 (1938), which held that the doctrine of Swift v. Tyson was (and always had been) unconstitutional, see Chapter 4 *infra*, text following note 52.

30. John Bannister Gibson (1780–1853) was chief justice of the Supreme Court of Pennsylvania from 1827 until his death; on Shaw, see Chapter 2 *supra*, note 28; on Kent, see Chapter 2 *supra*, note 14.

31. It has been pointed out to me that there are statutes that break new ground or authorize the creation of new institutions (corporations, administrative agencies, authorities of all kinds) and thus can hardly be considered as being in derogation of the past. The point is obviously well taken. The statement in the text refers to the general run of statutes which regulate civil liability.

32. *Stare decisis* (to stand by the decisions) is conventional legal shorthand for the idea that a court is bound, in deciding a current case, to follow its own past decisions in "like" cases. Which current cases are "like" which past cases is a point on which opposing counsel tend to disagree.

33. On the invalidation of social legislation by the state courts during the second half of the nineteenth century, see L. Friedman, *A History of American Law* 311 *et seq.* (1973). Two examples of the "freedom of contract" approach are Godcharles v. Wigeman,

113 Pa. St. 431, 6 Atl. 354 (1886) and Ritchie v. People, 115 Ill. 98, 40 N.E. 454 (1895). In the Godcharles case the Pennsylvania Court held unconstitutional a statute which required certain mining and manufacturing businesses to pay their employees at least once a month and to pay in cash or legal tender, not in scrip redeemable only at company stores, and it forbade overcharging at such stores (an attempt, said the Court, speaking of the statute as a whole, "to do what, in this country, cannot be done, that is, prevent persons who are *sui juris* from making their own contracts"). In the Ritchie case the Illinois Court, which had a long series of cases of this sort to its credit, invalidated a statute which restricted to eight hours a day and forty-eight hours a week the work of women in factories and "workshops" (a "purely arbitrary restriction upon the fundamental rights of the citizen to control his or her own time and faculties"). I have borrowed these examples from Professor Friedman's discussion, cited above. As late as 1911 the New York Court of Appeals invalidated a Workmen's Compensation Act which the legislature had enacted the previous year, Ives v. South Buffalo Ry. Co., 200 N.Y. 271, 94 N.E. 431 (1911). Professor Friedman makes the point that not all state courts shared the views of the Pennsylvania and Illinois courts, even in the 1880s and 1890s. By the time of World War I most courts had abandoned the extreme position illustrated by the cases which have been cited in this note. Note 36 *infra* discusses other cases of this type which were made notable by the dissents of Holmes, J. In the Supreme Court the conservative majority precipitated a constitutional crisis by its repeated invalidation of New Deal legislation in the early 1930s—a crisis which was eventually resolved, after the failure of President Roosevelt's court-packing plan, by changes in the Court's membership. The crisis, while it endured, called forth attacks by liberals on the entire institution of judicial review of legislative action; see, e.g., E. Corwin, *The Twilight of the Supreme Court* (1934); *Court over Constitution* (1938).

34. On these matters, see Chapter 2 *supra*.

35. Kessler, "Contracts of Adhesion—Some Thoughts about Freedom of Contract," 43 *Colum. L. Rev.* 629 (1943) may have been

the first expression of this idea in the American literature. It seems
to have become commonplace in the 1960s. See, among many examples which could be cited, L. Friedman, *Contract Law in America* 20–24 (1965); Farnsworth, "Legal Remedies for Breach of Contract," 70 *Colum. L. Rev.* 1145, 1216 (1970); G. Gilmore, *The Death
of Contract* 94 *et seq.* (1974). For an example from England, Atiyah,
An Introduction to the Law of Contract 3 (2d ed. 1971). Among
commentators who can be identified as liberals on the political
spectrum, the parallelism between late nineteenth-century legal
and economic theories is stressed to make the point that, in the late
twentieth century, neither the legal nor the economic theory seems
plausible. Conservative commentators, accepting the parallelism,
make the points that both laissez-faire economic theory and the
legal structure which echoed it were (and are) sound and that, to
the extent we have abandoned either, salvation lies in returning to
the true faith. Professor Richard Posner of the University of Chicago Law School has been an influential spokesman for this point
of view. See his "A Theory of Negligence," 1 *J. of Legal Studies* 29
(1972); also his book, *Economic Analysis of Law* (1973). For a critical review of the book, see Leff, "Economic Analysis of Law: Some
Realism about Nominalism," 60 *Va. L. Rev.* 451 (1974).

36. See text at and following note 15 *supra*. See, among the many
illustrations that could be put forward, Holmes's celebrated dissent
in Lochner v. New York, 198 U.S. 45 (1905) in which the Court
invalidated a New York Statute which limited employment in bak-
eries to sixty hours a week and ten hours a day. The majority held
that the statute was an arbitrary interference with the right of freedom to contract, guaranteed by the Fourteenth Amendment to the
federal Constitution. Holmes, referring to the "right of a majority to embody their opinions in law," commented: "I think that the
word liberty in the Fourteenth Amendment is perverted when it
is held to prevent the natural outcome of a dominant opinion . . ."
(At p. 76 of 198 U.S.) See also his dissent in Coppage v. Kansas,
236 U.S. 1, 26 (1914) in which the majority of the Court invalidated
a Kansas statute which prohibited so-called yellow dog contracts

(in which, as a condition of employment, workers were required to promise not to join a union). During his tenure on the Massachusetts Court, the majority of the Court held, in Vegelahn v. Guntner, 167 Mass. 92 (1896), that picketing by members of a striking union was illegal, even though the picketing was not accompanied by violence or the threat of violence: Holmes dissented in one of his most eloquent opinions, writing (at p. 108 of 167 Mass.): "One of the eternal conflicts out of which life is made up is that between the effort of every man to get the most he can for his services, and that of society, disguised under the name of capital, to get his services for the least possible return. Combination on the one side is patent and powerful, Combination on the other is the necessary and desirable counterpart, if the battle is to be carried on in a fair and equal way." In his dissent in Coppage v. Kansas, Holmes cited this passage of his dissent in Vegelahn v. Guntner. The Vegelahn dissent earned Holmes a reputation as a radical. When President Roosevelt nominated him for the Supreme Court in 1902, Holmes feared that that reputation might jeopardize his chances for confirmation. See his letters to Pollock of August 13, 1902, and September 23, 1902, in 1 *Holmes-Pollock Letters* 103, 106 (Howe ed. 1961).

CHAPTER 4

1. "The Papacy is not other than the Ghost of the deceased Roman Empire, sitting crowned upon the grave thereof." Hobbes, *Leviathan* Part IV, at 47 (1651).

2. On the survival of the Langdellian spirit, see text at and following note 44 *infra,* and text following note 8 to Chapter 5.

3. Brandeis (1856–1941) went into practice in Boston following his graduation from the Harvard Law School in 1878. His practice, which was originally of a perfectly conventional nature, gradually involved him, on a national scale, with the great social and political problems of the day, and he became known as the most effective advocate of liberal or progressive ideology. Nominated to the Supreme Court by President Wilson in 1916, he was bitterly attacked

by conservatives in the Senate hearings, but his appointment was eventually confirmed by a 47–22 vote. He served as an Associate Justice until his retirement in 1939.

4. Pound (1870–1964) received a Ph.D. in botany from the University of Nebraska in 1897 but never received a law degree, although he had studied law at Harvard for a year (1889–1890). He was admitted to the Nebraska bar and practiced law while teaching botany at the University of Nebraska. He was a professor of law at Harvard from 1910 to 1937 and served as dean from 1916 to 1936. For his advocacy of sociological jurisprudence, see his series of articles under the general title "The Scope and Purpose of Sociological Jurisprudence," 24 *Harv. L. Rev.* 591 (1912); 25 *id.* 140 (1912); 25 *id.* 489 (1912). The term "sociological jurisprudence," at that time, had little or nothing to do with the theories of academic sociologists; Pound and others used the term to mean an approach to law under which judges could and should weigh in the balance the social and economic consequences of their decisions. Thus he was one of the first to attack the premises of what I have called Langdellian jurisprudence (see Chapter 3 *supra*). The irony of Pound's overlong career was that, long before his death, he had come to be considered an arch-reactionary. In the 1930s he became the principal butt of the Legal Realists under circumstances which are described in note 25 *infra*.

5. On the Progressive Movement, see R. Wiebe, *Businessmen and Reform: A Study of the Progressive Movement* (1962); R. Wiebe, *The Search for Order, 1877–1920* (1967); S. Wood, *Constitutional Politics in the Progressive Era: Child Labor and the Law* (1968).

6. On the pre–Civil War codification movement, see Chapter 2 *supra*, text at and following note 9.

7. The Negotiable Instruments Law, universally nicknamed the N.I.L., was promulgated in 1896 and eventually enacted in all American jurisdictions. The Uniform Sales Act, which never acquired a nickname, was promulgated in 1906 and enacted in 37 states (the non-enacting states were mostly in the South and Southwest). Other commercial law statutes drafted during this period covered bills of lading, warehouse receipts, the transfer of

share certificates, and conditional sales. All these statutes, including the N.I.L. and the Sales Act, were repealed in all enacting states when the Uniform Commercial Code was adopted. On the Code see §III of this chapter.

8. On Langdell and his ideas, see Chapter 3 *supra*.

9. On Swift v. Tyson, see Chapter 2 *supra*, text following note 18. Some examples of the nationally acceptable solutions which the device produced are collected in note 24 to Chapter 2.

10. Commissions to codify the common law (including the law of contracts) were established by the Law Commissions Act 1965. Hahlo, in "Codifying the Common Law: Protracted Gestation," 38 *Mod. L. Rev.* 23, 26 (1975), commented that "the prospect of a codification of the law of contracts has receded into the nebulous future" and added that "Codes of the law of torts and the law of restitution lie unformed in the womb of time."

11. James Barr Ames (1846–1910) was appointed to the faculty of the Harvard Law School in 1873, became dean, succeeding Langdell, in 1895, and served in that office until shortly before his death. On Ames, see Chapter VII of A. Sutherland, *The Law at Harvard* (1967). Moot court arguments at the Harvard Law School are based on hypothetical cases which arise in the State of Ames (or, if a municipal ordinance is involved, in the City of Langdell). I do not know when the Harvards adopted this engaging practice but I know that it was in use in the 1960s.

12. S. Williston, *The Law Governing Sales of Goods at Common Law and under the Uniform Sales Act* (1909). The latest and, presumably, last edition of the sales treatise appeared, in four volumes, in 1948. The comment in the text is based on my own reading of the Sales Act case law while teaching the course on sales in several law schools over a good many years. Williston (1861–1963) was a member of the Harvard Law School faculty from 1890 to 1938. In addition to his treatise on sales he wrote a treatise on contracts which was first published in 1920. He was the Chief Reporter for the Restatement of Contracts; the Restatement project is discussed in the following passage of the text. Williston was one of the best statutory draftsmen who has ever worked at that mysterious art; he

was the most ingenious system-builder in the history of our jurisprudence; he wrote with lucidity and grace.

13. The founder and guiding spirit of the Institute and the Restatement project was William Draper Lewis, dean of the University of Pennsylvania Law School. See Goodrich, "The Story of the American Law Institute," 1951 *Wash. U. L.Q.* 283. Judge Herbert Goodrich, the author of the article cited, succeeded Dean Lewis as director of the Institute.

14. See Chapter 1 *supra*, text following note 4.

15. Indeed the Restatements, which had apparently been conceived as formulations good for all time, endured, in their original form, for not much more than a generation. Since the 1950s the American Law Institute has been at work producing a "Second Series" of Restatements. I have commented on some of the provisions of the (still unfinished) Second Restatement of Contracts in Chapter III, text following note 163, of *The Death of Contract* (1974).

16. Cardozo (1870–1938) studied law at Columbia and practiced in New York City from 1891 until he was elected to the New York Supreme Court in 1913. Promoted to the Court of Appeals (the court of last resort in the New York system) the following year, he served on that court until his appointment to the Supreme Court of the United States in 1932.

17. See, e.g., B. Shientag, *The Seventy-Fifth Anniversary of the Birth of Justice Benjamin N. Cardozo* 1–2 (1945): "What words are there to describe the charm of an uncommon gentleness, of a singular simplicity that goes with spiritual distinction; to picture that candor, that rare integrity and purity of mind, that life of intellectual opulence and moral fervor? What words have we to adumbrate that exquisite grace of humility, that abiding serenity, that intense tenderness and compassion which flowed from having himself suffered?"

18. See, e.g., Allegheny College v. National Chautauqua County Bank, 246 N.Y. 369, 379, 159 N.E. 173, 177 (1927) (Kellogg, J., dissenting); Jacob & Youngs, Inc. v. Kent, 230 N.Y. 239, 245, 129 N.E. 889, 892 (1921) (McLaughlin, J., dissenting); MacPherson v. Buick Motor Co., 217 N.Y. 382, 395, 111 N.E. 1050, 1055 (1916)

(Bartlett, C. J., dissenting). The Allegheny College case involved the law of charitable subscriptions; Jacob and Youngs involved the so-called rule of substantial performance in construction contracts; the MacPherson case involved a manufacturer's liability to a remote buyer for a defectively manufactured product. In all three cases Cardozo, writing the majority opinions, imposed liability on defendants who would almost certainly (with the possible exception of the Allegheny College case) not have been held liable if anyone but Cardozo had been stating and analyzing the prior case law which the majority opinions purported to follow.

19. See, e.g., Comfort v. McCorkle, 149 Misc. 826, 268 N.Y.S. 192 (Sup. Ct. 1933). The plaintiff had suffered a fire loss. The defendant, agent of the insurance company with which plaintiff carried his fire insurance, promised the plaintiff that he (the agent) would file proof of loss. No proof was filed within the required period and as a result the insurance company was discharged from liability on the policy. In an action against the agent, judgment was for the defendant. The result was not only a miscarriage of justice but also a completely unnecessary misreading of Cardozo's Allegheny College opinion, note 18 *supra*.

20. On *The Common Law*, see Chapter 3 *supra*, text following note 18. *The Nature of the Judicial Process* was published in 1921.

21. See note 4 *supra* for this use of the term "sociological jurisprudence" in the early part of the twentieth century.

22. *The Nature of the Judicial Process* 166–167 (1921).

23. Professor Arthur Corbin, who had been responsible for Cardozo's giving the lectures at Yale, wrote: "[Cardozo] was aware that his conception of the judicial process was not the generally accepted one; and he had a slight hesitation about the publication of his lectures. With a touch of humor, he remarked, 'If I were to publish them I would be impeached.'" Corbin, Foreword to B. Cardozo, *The Growth of the Law*, at vi (1966).

24. W. Twining, *Karl Llewellyn and the Realist Movement* (1973). Professor Twining devotes the first five chapters of his book, plus a concluding chapter, to the Realist Movement. On Llewellyn, see Chapter 1 *supra*, note 11.

25. The law review controversy stemmed from a short article by Dean Pound of Harvard which he entitled "The Call for a Realist Jurisprudence," 44 *Harv. L. Rev.* 697 (1931). The issue of the *Law Review* in which the article appeared was dedicated to Justice Holmes, as a tribute to him on his ninetieth birthday. Pound had promised the editors a piece for their Holmes issue but had not had time to prepare one and gave them the piece on Realist Jurisprudence (which is the only item not related to Holmes in the entire issue) as a substitute. It is about fifteen pages long, has no footnotes, and shows every sign of having been hastily written (or perhaps dictated). Pound, after briefly mentioning the nineteenth-century schools of historical and analytical jurisprudence and the twentieth-century school of sociological jurisprudence with which he himself had been associated (see note 4 *supra*), said that a new school, which he called Realist Jurisprudence, seemed to be establishing itself. Without naming any of the members of the new "school," he then proceeded to a not unsympathetic analysis of what he identified as five principal characteristics of their writing.

Karl Llewellyn and Jerome Frank felt themselves to be the targets of what they regarded as Dean Pound's attack. Llewellyn, the previous year, had published an article which he called "A Realistic Jurisprudence—The Next Step," 30 *Colum. L. Rev.* 431 (1930), in the course of which he had made some less than flattering remarks about Pound. Frank may have felt that his recently published *Law and the Modern Mind* (1930) was what Pound was getting at. At all events Llewellyn and Frank jointly prepared a reply to Pound which was published, under Llewellyn's name, as "Some Realism about Realism—Responding to Dean Pound," 44 *Harv. L. Rev.* 1222 (1931). Identifying themselves (and a number of others) as "Realists," they argued, vehemently and at length, that Pound had totally misconceived what they had been saying and that none of Pound's five "characteristics" could be properly applied to their work. They ended by denying that there was anything that could be properly described as a "school" of realist jurisprudence—which seemed inconsistent with their identification of themselves as Realists.

The absurd truth appears to be that Pound had not had either Llewellyn or Frank in mind; it is entirely possible that he had never read anything by either of them. Thus it was quite true that his five "characteristics" had only an accidental or remote application to the work of Llewellyn or Frank (or most of the other people whom they co-opted as "Realists"). In his hastily written piece Pound was, in all probability, commenting on trends he had noticed in recent legal writing without having any individual or group in mind. He was, apparently, mystified by their attack on him.

From this tissue of misunderstandings came the celebrated controversy about Legal Realism—which, before it had finally run its course in the late 1930s, accounted for hundreds, if not thousands, of tedious pages in the law reviews. The saddest part of the story is that Dean Pound, who had been one of the earliest and most effective spokesmen in the reaction against Langdellian formalism, ended up as the favorite whipping-boy of the new school (or non-school or anti-school). Thus the reputation of a man who had made a notable contribution to our jurisprudence was unfairly tarnished—which was a great loss to all of us, including the Realists themselves.

Professor Paul Freund, who was president of the *Harvard Law Review* when the Holmes issue was published in 1931, has confirmed the foregoing account of an exchange which he characterizes as having had a "sadly comic" quality.

26. Indeed Llewellyn was accustomed to describe his own writings as examples of what the new jurisprudence was about. In a note on "Realism and Method" in *The Common Law Tradition: Deciding Appeals* 508 *et seq.* (1960) he wrote (at p. 512): "I therefore claim to know what it ["Realistic jurisprudence"] was about and what it is about. I now put forward, explicitly as a proper product and exhibit of *real* realism, this book." (Emphasis in original.) In 1960 Llewellyn read a draft of a piece of mine which appeared as "Legal Realism: Its Cause and Cure," 70 *Yale L.J.* 1037 (1961). He commented: "Where you all go wrong is in thinking that Realism was a theory. It was not. It was merely a methodology."

27. See Chapter 3 *supra,* text at and following note 2.

28. Arthur Linton Corbin (1874–1967) took his law degree at Yale and then practiced law briefly in Cripple Creek, Colorado. He spent the rest of his career teaching law at Yale. He published many law review articles on the law of contracts; his treatise on contracts appeared in 1950. I am on record as having described the Corbin treatise as "the greatest law book ever written" (*The Death of Contract* 57 (1974)). I was Professor Corbin's student and later, as a junior member of the Yale faculty, benefited greatly from his wise counsel.

29. The first edition of Williston's treatise, *The Law of Contracts,* appeared in 1920. On the relationship between Corbin and Williston, see Corbin, "Samuel Williston," 76 *Harv. L. Rev.* 1327 (1963), a moving tribute written after Williston's death when Corbin himself was almost ninety. On Williston, see note 12 *supra.*

30. 1 A. Corbin, *Contracts* §110, at 494 (1963): "In each new case, the question for the court is 'should this promise be enforced.' Its problem is not merely to determine mechanically, or logically, whether it falls within Professor Wiseacre's statement of the doctrine of consideration or complies with some commonly repeated definition. This is not to say that the Professor's statement, or Restatement, or the learned judge's dictum, can be safely disregarded."

There can be no doubt that "Professor Wiseacre" was Williston. I assume that the "learned judge" was Holmes.

On the battle between Corbin and Williston over the definition of "consideration" to be adopted in the Restatement of Contracts, see my discussion in *The Death of Contract* 62 *et seq.* (1974).

31. Wesley Alba Sturges (1893–1962) took his law degree at Columbia and spent most of his professional career teaching at the Yale Law School, serving as dean 1945–1954. By way of explaining why his students revered him, I will retell an anecdote which I used in an obituary piece which I called "For Wesley Sturges: On the Teaching and Study of Law," 72 *Yale L.J.* 646 (1963). In the fall of 1941 a number of students (of whom I was one) came to the odd

conclusion that our legal education would not be complete without a course in the common law forms of action—a subject which, then as now, did not make the grade in the forward-looking curriculum of the Yale Law School. I quote from 72 *Yale L.J.* at pp. 646, 654: "We decided to ask Wesley Sturges to offer such a course in the spring term. When our delegation waited on him his attitude was one of grave courtesy and mild amusement: he neither commended us for our historical interest, nor castigated us for having lost touch with reality. He would, he said, offer the course if a sufficient number of students signed up. He did not point out to us that, in addition to his having a full teaching schedule for the spring term, he had committed a large portion of his time to activities on behalf of both the state and federal governments in connection with what was called, before Pearl Harbor, the defense effort. The course was announced, about twenty students signed up and, through the catastrophic spring of 1942, Wesley labored patiently with us as we canvased the mysteries of replevin, trover, detinue, and debt. . . . What did Wesley teach us? He taught us, in a way that none of us will ever forget, something—indeed a great deal—about the use and the uses of words. I can think of few things that are more central to the lawyer's craft and art. He taught us to be forever on our guard against the slippery generality, the received principle, the authoritative proposition. He taught us to trust no one's judgment except our own—and not to be too sure of that. He taught us how to live by our wits. He taught us, in a word, how to be lawyers."

32. Sturges, "Legal Theory and Real Property Mortgages," 37 *Yale L.J.* 691 (1928). I discussed the article in the obituary piece, note 31 *supra,* 72 *Yale L.J.* at p. 651 *et seq.*

33. W. Sturges, *The Law of Credit Transactions* (1930).

34. Nothing, that is, on conventional law or legal theory. He became interested in arbitration as a promising alternative to judicial adjudication and published a comprehensive treatise on that subject, W. Sturges, *A Treatise on Commercial Arbitrations and Awards* (1930).

35. On Llewellyn, see Chapter 1 *supra*, note 11; on Llewellyn and Legal Realism, see note 25 *supra* and the accompanying text. On pre-Langdellian pluralism, see Chapter 3 *supra*, text following note 6. For another example of the return toward pluralism during this period, see Kessler, "Contracts of Adhesion—Some Thoughts about Freedom of Contract," 43 *Colum. L. Rev.* 629 (1943), which I have discussed in a tribute to Kessler, 84 *Yale L.J.* 672 (1975).

36. See "On Warranty of Quality, and Society," 36 *Colum. L. Rev.* 699 (1936), 37 *id.* 341 (1937); "Through Title to Contract and a Bit Beyond," 3 *Law—A Century of Progress* 80 (1937), reprinted 15 *N.Y.U. L.Q. Rev.* 159 (1938); "Across Sales on Horseback," 52 *Harv. L. Rev.* 725 (1939). The casebook, *Cases and Materials on Sales* (1930), was not a success in the academic marketplace and never appeared in a second edition. I have been told that it was "unteachable" (except, of course, when Llewellyn was doing the teaching). However, in the late 1940s it was the indispensable reference tool for any young instructor assigned to teach the sales course. I know it was for me.

37. On what Holmes meant by a "philosophically continuous series," see Chapter 3 *supra*, text at note 21.

38. On the genesis of the Code project, see W. Twining, *Karl Llewellyn and the Realist Movement* (1973). Drafting on what became the Code started in the late 1930s. I became a member of the drafting staff in 1946 and served until the staff was disbanded in 1954. I subsequently served as a member of or as a consultant to committees charged with considering revisions of Article 9 (on Secured Transactions). The following discussion of the Code is based on my own memory of what went on.

Danzig's "A Comment on the Jurisprudence of the Uniform Commercial Code," 27 *Stan. L. Rev.* 621 (1975), is an interesting attempt to relate Llewellyn's jurisprudential ideas, as he expressed them in *The Common Law Tradition: Deciding Appeals* (1960), with the style and substance of the Code (particularly Article 2 on Sales). Professor Danzig emphasizes the open-endedness of the Code's drafting (i.e., the frequent use of such undefined and undefinable terms as "commercial reasonableness," "good faith," and so on). In the following discussion in the text I refer to Llewellyn's concept of a "case law code," which would abolish the past without attempting to control the future. That concept seems to be the same one that Professor Danzig identifies in his comments on the Article 2 drafting. Professor Danzig, who appears to disapprove of this open-ended style of drafting, is, I believe, correct in drawing attention to the extent to which the style survived even in the final draft of Article 2. If he had included other articles of the Code (particularly Article 9 on Secured Transactions) in his analysis, he would, I am quite sure, have found much less open-endedness to complain about. By the time Article 9 was drafted the proponents of a much tighter style of drafting had taken charge. On the subsequent history of Article 9, see note 56 *infra*.

39. On the earlier codification of commercial law, see text following note 6 *supra*.

40. On the Restatements, see text at and following note 13 *supra*.

41. In the 1920s he had drafted for the Conference a Uniform Chattel Mortgage Act which, despite much merit, was not enacted anywhere. In the early 1930s he had drafted the Uniform Trust Receipts Act, which was widely enacted. On the Trust Receipts Act, see 1 G. Gilmore, *Security Interests in Personal Property*, Chapter 7 (1965).

42. On post–World War II judicial activism, see §V *infra*. The products liability cases, discussed in note 48 *infra* as an example of activism on the state court level in a private law area, effectively nullified the apparent victory of the conservatives in procuring the deletion of the proposed Code provisions which would have increased the liability of manufacturers for defective goods.

43. I was a law student myself in the early 1940s. I testify to what I witnessed.

44. The thesis of Carl Becker, *The Heavenly City of the Eighteenth-Century Philosophers* (1931), is that, despite their rhetorical attacks on church and state, Voltaire and the other "philosophes" in effect

accepted the basic tenets of the ideology which they professed to despise. If I am right, the Realists and the Langdellians also shared a community of interest. See my comments, text at and following note 1 *supra*.

45. See Chapter 3 *supra*, text at note 2.

46. See Lasswell and McDougal, "Legal Education and Public Policy: Professional Training in the Public Interest," 52 *Yale L.J.* 203 (1943); McDougal, "The Law School of the Future: From Legal Realism to Policy Science in the World Community," 56 *Yale L.J.* 1345 (1947). After World War II Professor McDougal, whose initial field of specialization had been property law, turned to international law. With various collaborators he has produced a series of volumes on international law subjects in which he applies the theoretical insights on which his policy science system is based.

47. On the Progressive Movement, see note 5 *supra*.

48. On the Supreme Court itself the formation of a usually reliable activist majority for which Justices Black and Douglas were frequently the spokesmen dates from the 1940s. See the discussion in the text following note 53 *infra* of the growth of what has been called the New Federalism. One area in which that majority completely rewrote the law during the 1940s was that of recovery for death and injury for seamen and other maritime workers, see G. Gilmore and C. Black, *The Law of Admiralty*, 272 *et seq.* (2d ed. 1975). The most dramatic example of activism on the state court level in a private law field since World War II has been the imposition of "strict" (or no-fault) liability on manufacturers toward those who may be injured by the use of defective products. The strict liability idea, in whose formulation the California Supreme Court played a pioneering role (see Greenman v. Yuba Power Products, Inc., 59 Cal. 2d 57, 377 P. 2d 897 (1962)), had, in less than ten years, been widely adopted throughout the country and was accepted in §402A of the Second Restatement of Torts. On the products liability cases, which have generated an enormous literature, see the symposium "Products Liability: Economic Analysis and the Law," 38 *U. of Chi. L. Rev.* 1 (1970), in which the strict liability idea is

attacked by some economists and lawyers but defended by others (including myself).

49. I do not mean that judicial activism will necessarily be our permanent state. See the discussion of what has been called the New Conceptualism in Chapter 5 *infra*, text following note 7.

50. See Chapter 3 *supra*, text following note 30.

51. I have traced this process in the area of contract law in Chapters III and IV of *The Death of Contract* (1974).

52. Erie R.R. v. Tompkins, 304 U.S. 64 (1938), per Brandeis, J. On Swift v. Tyson, see Chapter 2 *supra*, text following note 18. On the decline of the Swift v. Tyson device, see Chapter 3 *supra*, text following note 28.

53. One of the earliest discussions of the post-*Erie* federalization was in Judge Henry Friendly's 1964 Cardozo lecture to the Association of the Bar of the City of New York, "In Praise of *Erie*— and of the New Federal Common Law," reprinted 39 *N.Y.U. L. Rev.* 383 (1964). For a review of the process in various fields, see 1 G. Gilmore, *Security Interests in Personal Property*, Chapter 13 (1965).

54. The federal supremacy idea received its most extensive development in the maritime injury and death cases, starting with Garrett v. Moore-McCormack Co., Inc., 317 U.S. 239 (1942). The long sequence of Supreme Court admiralty cases of this type is discussed in G. Gilmore and C. Black, *The Law of Admiralty*, §6–59 *et seq.* (2d ed. 1975). When a court talks of fashioning a federal rule where none previously existed, what is usually meant is that the court is choosing between conflicting rules which have established themselves on the state level or (as the Supreme Court used to do in the nineteenth century under Swift v. Tyson) arriving at a new synthesis derived from the conflicting rules. That is, the rule-fashioning process uses existing materials or recombines them; almost never is the new federal rule a radical departure.

55. Although, in the early days, the state courts did in fact adopt the federal rule more often than not. For an example, see Chapter 2 *supra*, note 23.

56. See my comments on the drafting history of the Uniform Commercial Code, text at and following note 42 *supra*. Indeed the tensions revealed by the developing case law under Article 9 of the Code (Secured Transactions) had become so acute by the late 1960s that the sponsoring organizations (see text at note 39 *supra*) undertook a revision of the article which was promulgated in 1972 and had, by 1976, been enacted in more than a dozen states. Thus we now have, and presumably will go on having, two versions of Article 9 in force—which is obviously destructive of the national uniformity in the law which the Code was designed to assure. Even so, the Article 9 story is a cause for rejoicing when we think of all the other statutes, state and federal, which are sorely in need of revision, have not been revised, and, in all probability, never will be revised.

57. Two celebrated examples of this process are the Elizabethan Statute of Fraudulent Conveyances (1570) and the Carolingian Statute of Frauds (1677). The dates of the statutes suggest how long the process takes.

58. The idea of this approach to the problem of statutory obsolescence was first suggested to me by a series of maritime industrial accident cases which the Supreme Court of the United States decided during the 1950s and 1960s. These cases involved both the Jones Act (46 U.S.C. §688), a 1920 statute under which "seamen" (or their representatives) may recover for death or injury caused by "negligence" attributable to their employers, and the Longshoremen's and Harbor Workers' Compensation Act of 1927 (33 U.S.C. §901 *et seq.*), under which the employers of maritime workers (other than "seamen") were to be liable to their employees only for compensation under the act (and not for the damages recoverable in a tort action). By 1970 the Court had in effect nullified both the negligence requirement of the Jones Act and the exclusive liability provision of the Compensation Act; thus both seamen and other harbor workers could recover full damages without proving negligence. (1972 amendments to the Compensation Act were designed to overturn much of what the Court had done in the harbor worker

cases.) For a full discussion of these developments, see G. Gilmore and C. Black, *The Law of Admiralty*, Chapter VI, particularly §6–56 (2d ed. 1975).

I wrote the passage in the text in 1974 with the maritime industrial accident cases in mind, speculating that state courts might well begin to treat the turn of the century Workmen's Compensation Acts in the same way that the Supreme Court had treated the federal act.

Since 1974 the California Supreme Court has provided a dramatic example of statutory nullification in Li v. Yellow Cab Co., 13 Cal. 3d 804, 119 Cal. Reptr. 858, 532 P. 2d 1226 (1975). The Court concluded that the California Civil Code of 1872 had adopted the common law contributory negligence rule (plaintiff's negligence, however slight, bars any recovery), took note of the fact that the California legislature had refused to amend the Code provision and held that, despite the Code, California would now adopt a "comparative negligence" rule (plaintiff's negligence will be taken into account in assessing damages but will not bar recovery). Courts in several other states have commented on the holding in the Li case without betraying any visible signs of shock or outrage.

59. As had been the case with the problem of statutory obsolescence (see note 58 *supra*), my attention was drawn to the problem of obsolete Supreme Court cases by some recent admiralty litigation. There are many areas of admiralty law in which the Supreme Court has not decided a case since the 1920s or even earlier, so that the problem of obsolescence has become acute. See Petition of Chadade Steamship Co., Inc. (The Yarmouth Castle), 266 F. Supp. 517 (S.D. Fla. 1967) for a case in which, arguably, Judge Mehrtens, a highly respected admiralty judge, came "perilously close" to overruling (or refusing to follow) The Titanic, 233 U.S. 718 (1914). G. Gilmore and C. Black, *The Law of Admiralty*, 943–944 (2d ed. 1975).

Having reached this point in my own thinking, I was fascinated to come across a Note, "Lower Court Disavowal of Supreme Court Precedent," 60 *Va. L. Rev.* 494 (1974), which contains an elaborate,

and excellent, discussion. The writer of the Note properly emphasizes, in addition to the problem of obsolescence, the problems created by the erosion of precedent during the period since the 1940s
when the Supreme Court has been dominated, most of the time,
by an activist majority. He also makes the interesting suggestion
that the general decline in respect for precedent can be traced back
to the Realist attack on formalism, citing White, "The Evolution
of Reasoned Elaboration: Jurisprudential Criticism and Social
Change," 59 *Va. L. Rev.* 279 (1973).

Evidently, these ideas are in the air. We shall, no doubt, hear
more of them.

CHAPTER 5

1. See Chapter 1 *supra*, §II, where the eighteenth-century origins of the hypothesis are discussed.

2. See Chapter 4 *supra*, §IV.

3. The passage in the text is borrowed from "The Age of Antiquarius: On Legal History in a Time of Troubles," 39 *U. of Chi. L.
Rev.* 475 (1972), a paper which I delivered as the inaugural William Winslow Crosskey Lecture in Legal History at the University
of Chicago Law School.

4. I have been told that large law firms already find it worth their
while to subscribe to such computerized services, which do not
come cheap. The present systems will, no doubt, seem outmoded
and primitive within a few years.

5. On Llewellyn's historical work, see, in addition to *The Common Law Tradition: Deciding Appeals* (1960), his casebook and articles on sales law which are discussed in Chapter 4 *supra*, text at
and following note 36. On the historical thesis of *The Common Law
Tradition*, see Chapter 1 *supra*, §IV.

6. I have deliberately used the cumbersome phrase "what has
come to be called legal history" in order to give myself the opportunity to express my disapproval of the term "legal history." The only
legal materials that are or ever have been or ever will be available
are historical—cases that have already been decided, statutes that

have already been enacted, and so on. There is absolutely no point in setting up a separate category of legal writing (or law teaching) to be known as "legal history." To the extent that we segregate the study of our legal past from the study of our legal present, we become not historians but antiquarians.

7. The emphasis on procedural regularity and the following of precedents in the academic version of the Rule of Law idea suggests that we are dealing with a survival (or revival) of nineteenth-century formalism. I do not know exactly when the Rule of Law tag, as a shorthand expression for these ideas, came into use or who first used it. My best memory is that the tag had acquired the exalted status of a cliché by the mid-1950s. The people who promoted the Rule of Law in the 1950s may be taken as forerunners of the New Conceptualists of the 1970s, whose work will presently be discussed in the text.

8. See, however, the final paragraph of note 11 *infra*.

9. *The Death of Contract* 103 (1974).

10. See Chapter 4 *supra*, §III.

11. See, for example, the work of Professor Richard Posner of the University of Chicago Law School, two examples of which are cited Chapter 3 *supra*, note 35. The *Journal of Legal Studies*, which Professor Posner has edited since it was founded in 1972, has published a great deal of material of this sort. At the end of the second issue Professor Posner contributed an Afterword in which he explained the purpose of the editors: "The aim of the *Journal* is to encourage the application of scientific methods to the study of the legal system. As biology is to living organisms, astronomy to the stars, or economics to the price system, so should legal studies be to the legal system: an endeavor to make precise, objective, and systematic observations of how the legal system operates in fact and to discover and explain the recurrent patterns in the observations—the 'laws' of the system." (Posner, "Volume One of the Journal of Legal Studies—An Afterword," 1 *J. Legal Studies* 437 (1972). Cf. the remarks of Dean Langdell in 1886, quoted Chapter 3 *supra*, text at note 2.

As another example of the New Conceptualism, I would cite the extremely interesting work of Professor Ian Macneil. See, e.g., "The

Many Futures of Contracts," 47 *S. Calif. L. Rev.* 691 (1974). I understand that the article cited is the first instalment of (or a precursor to) a major work on contract theory.

Some of the reviews of my lectures, *The Death of Contract* (1974), also seem to me to have been animated by the spirit of the New Conceptualism. See, e.g., the review by Gordley, 89 *Harv. L. Rev.* 452 (1975), in the course of which the author comments (at p. 455): "Professor Gilmore's book is as full of unconscious historical forces as Cotton Mather's book is of spirits riding invisibly on wind and water," citing C. Mather, *The Wonders of the Invisible World* (1693). Evidently the game of "Who's a Conceptualist?" is one that two can play. See also Mooney, "The Rise and Fall of Classical Contract Law: A Response to Professor Gilmore," 55 *Ore. L. Rev.* 155 (1976). Professor Mooney does me the great honor of accurately stating my ideas before proceeding, quite properly, to attack them. He collects the citations of other reviews in which the merits of my thesis have been questioned. For my own unrepentant views, see Chapter 3 *supra*, note 8.

My linking of the New Conceptualism with the "conservative reaction which inspired the political slogans [of the 1950s]" may not be altogether accurate. Much of the recent writing which I would lump under that rubric does seem to proceed from the extreme right wing (speaking both politically and jurisprudentially) but by no means all of it. Certainly, a fondness for unitary theory and universal abstraction has never been the exclusive possession of conservative thinkers. See, for an obvious example, the work of the late Karl Marx.

12. See Chapter 3 *supra*, text at note 16.

CHAPTER 6

1. See Grant Gilmore, *The Ages of American Law* 110 (2d ed., 2014) ("The values of a reasonably just society will reflect themselves in a reasonably just law.").

2. Patient Protection and Affordable Care Act, Pub. L. No. 111–148, 124 Stat. 119 (2010).

3. United States v. Windsor, 133 S. Ct. 2675, 2696 (2013).

4. Gilmore, *supra* note 1, at 110.

5. Paul A. Freund, *Mark DeWolfe Howe,* 79 Proceedings of the Mass. Hist. Soc'y, no. 1, 2008, at 198.

6. See Anthony Jon Waters, "For Grant Gilmore," 42 *Md. L. Rev.* 864, 871 n.22 (1983); "Memorial for Grant Gilmore," *N.Y. Times,* Sept. 29, 1982, http://www.nytimes.com/1982/09/29/obituaries/memorial-for-grant-gilmore.html.

7. "If law is not determinate or neutral or a function of reason and logic rather than values and politics, government by law reduces to government by lawyers, and there is little justification for the broad-scale displacement of democracy. The extraordinary role of law in our society and culture is hard to justify once the idealized model is recognized as mythic." David Kairys, "Introduction," in *The Politics of Law: A Progressive Critique* 5–6 (David Kairys ed., 3d ed. 1998).

8. Philip Bobbitt, *Constitutional Fate: Theory of the Constitution* 57 (1982).

9. *Id.* at 26; see also Leslie Friedman Goldstein, *In Defense of the Text: Democracy and Constitutional Theory* 191 (1991).

10. See Bobbitt, *supra* note 8, at 81–83.

11. See William Crosskey, *Politics and the Constitution in the History of the United States* 5 (1953) (explaining need to build "specialized dictionary" of word usages from time of ratifiers to understand Constitution).

12. See Bobbitt, *supra* note 8, at 13–14.

13. *Id.* at 61.

14. See John Rawls, *A Theory of Justice* 16–17 (rev. ed. 1999) (arguing that individuals reach just decisions when stripped of personal knowledge).

15. See Stephen Guest, *Ronald Dworkin* 213–14 (3d ed. 2013) (explaining Dworkin's adaptation of Rawls's approach).

16. See Akhil Amar, *America's Constitution: A Biography* (2005).

17. "From Mythology" by Zbigniew Herbert, from *Postwar Polish Poetry,* translated by Czeslaw Milosz. Copyright © 1965,

1983 by Czeslaw Milosz, used by permission of The Wylie Agency LLC.

18. Martin Garbus, Letter to the Editor, *Law and Politics, N.Y. Times,* May 23, 2013, http://www.nytimes.com/2013/05/26/books/review/law-and-politics.html. Garbus cited Edwin Meese for this observation.

19. Gilmore, *supra* note 1, at 107–08.

20. Joseph A. Schumpeter, *Capitalism, Socialism, and Democracy* 243 (5th ed. 1976).

21. Richard A. Posner, "Guido Calabresi's The Costs of Accidents: A Reassessment," 64 *Md. L. Rev.* 12, 14 (2005) (noting the "landmark status" of Calabresi's book).

22. Guido Calabresi, *The Costs of Accidents: A Legal and Economic Analysis* 79 (1970); see also Guido Calabresi, "About Law and Economics: A Letter to Ronald Dworkin," 8 *Hofstra L. Rev.* 553, 556–59 (1980) (distinguishing between discussions of justice and discussions of efficiency and wealth distribution).

23. Arthur Allen Leff, "Economic Analysis of Law: Some Realism About Nominalism," 60 *Va. L. Rev.* 451, 452 (1974).

24. Barbara Black, "Behavioral Economics and Investor Protection: Reasonable Investors, Efficient Markets," 44 *Loy. U. Chi. L.J.* 1493, 1499 (2013) ("In efficient markets, securities prices fully reflect available information. . . ."). It may also be worth noting that, in Halliburton v. Erica John Fund, the Supreme Court could have reversed its adoption of the efficient market hypothesis on which it relied in Basic v. Levinson, 485 U.S. 224 (1988); see http://online.wsj.com/news/articles/SB10001424052702303559504579200283202859124. Unanimously, the justices declined to do so. See No. 13-317 (U.S. June 23, 2014).

25. John F. Muth, "Rational Expectations and the Theory of Price Movements," 29 *Econometrica* 315, 316 (1961) ("[E]xpectations of firms (or, more generally, the subjective probability distribution of outcomes) tend to be distributed, for the same information set, about the prediction of the theory (or the 'objective' probability distributions of outcomes).").

26. See Samuel Dupernex, "Why Might Share Prices Follow a Random Walk?," 21 *Student Econ. Rev.* 167, 167–68 (2007) (defining random walk hypothesis).

27. See *Efficient Market Hypothesis-EMH,* Investopedia, http://www.investopedia.com/terms/e/efficientmarkethypothesis.asp (last visited Nov. 25, 2013) (defining efficient market hypothesis).

28. See *Hyperinflation,* Investopedia, http://www.investopedia.com/terms/h/hyperinflation.asp (last visited Nov. 25, 2013) (defining hyperinflation).

29. See *Permanent Income Hypothesis,* Investopedia, http://www.investopedia.com/terms/p/permanent-income-hypothesis.asp (last visited Nov. 25, 2013) (defining permanent income hypothesis).

30. See *Life-Cycle Hypothesis (LCH),* Investopedia, http://www.investopedia.com/terms/l/life-cycle-hypothesis.asp (last visited Nov. 25, 2013) (defining life-cycle hypothesis).

31. See, e.g., Richard A. Posner, "The Ethical and Political Basis of the Efficiency Norm in Common Law Adjudication," 8 *Hofstra L. Rev.* 487, 488–90 (1980) (discussing utilitarian and Kantian theories of "Pareto ethics"). But see Lawrence G. Sager, "Pareto Superiority, Consent, and Justice," 8 *Hofstra L. Rev.* 913 (1980) (questioning these theories). One state may be described as Pareto Superior to another if it makes at least one party better off and no party worse off. Pareto Superiority may be contrasted with Pareto Optimality, which means that it is impossible to make some parties better off without making others worse off. *Id.* at 914. Within economics, Pareto Superiority and Pareto Optimality are descriptive terms, but their proponents in law and economics have argued that they have normative weight as well. See Posner, *supra.*

32. R. H. Coase, "The Problem of Social Cost," 3 *J.L. & Econ.* 1 (1960). But (because of distributive consequences and wealth effects) it may be that the efficient allocation involves different material uses depending on the choice of legal rule. For a concrete example, imagine that a residence sits beside a factory. The law must decide whether the homeowner is entitled to quiet or the factory is entitled to make noise. If the factory is entitled to make noise, then

the homeowner may find it worthwhile to pay the factory to shut down at night. But having made the payment, she must be out at work all day earning money and anyway leads a spare existence at home. So it is not worthwhile to her to pay for quiet in the day also. So the factory operates in the day and shuts down at night, and that is efficient. Alternatively, suppose that the homeowner is entitled to quiet. Now she gets quiet at night for free, and being richer, she works less and fills her home with expensive hi-fi equipment, which she likes listening to. On account of this, the factory can no longer afford to pay her for the right to make noise even in the day. So the factory operates neither night nor day, and that is efficient. I am indebted to Daniel Markovits for this cogent and imaginative qualification.

33. "Suppose, Coase's argument suggested, that a railroad runs next to a farmer's field and that trains emit sparks that destroy the crops nearest the track. Suppose, too, that it would cost the railroad a hundred dollars to install a mechanism to prevent the sparks from flying, but the ruined crops are worth only fifty dollars to the farmer. Traditionally, a legal thinker might consider this a case of conflicting property rights, and would decide that the railroad's right to full use of the track trumped the farmer's right to full use of his land, or vice versa, leaving the loser worse off. But, Coase pointed out, it would be more efficient for the railroad to pay the farmer, say, sixty dollars for a right to emit sparks: that way the railroad would pay out sixty dollars instead of the hundred dollars it would have cost to install anti-spark mechanisms, and the farmer would profit sixty dollars from the land rather than fifty, and both would be better off." Larissa MacFarquhar, *The Bench Burner, The New Yorker,* Dec. 10, 2001, at 78, 86 (profiling Judge Richard Posner).

34. Oliver Wendell Holmes, Jr., *The Common Law* 50–51 (1881).

35. See Philip Bobbitt, *The Shield of Achilles: War, Peace, and the Course of History* (2002).

36. See www.scaruffi.com/politics/massacre.html.

37. Guy Gugliotta, "New Estimate Raises Civil War Death Toll," *N.Y. Times,* April 2, 2012, http://www.nytimes.com/2012/04/03/ science/civil-war-toll-up-by-20-percent-in-new-estimate.html.

38. *The Quotable Judge Posner: Selections from Twenty-Five Years of Judicial Opinions* 3 (Robert F. Blomquist ed., 2010).

39. MacFarquhar, *supra* note 33, at 88.

40. Richard A. Posner, *Economic Analysis of Law* (8th ed. 2011).

41. Fred Shapiro, "The Most-Cited Legal Scholars," 29 *J. Legal Stud.* 409, 424 tbl.6 (2000).

42. MacFarquhar, *supra* note 33, at 84.

43. Grant Gilmore, "Some Reflections on Oliver Wendell Holmes, Jr.," 2 *Green Bag* 379, 381 n.11 (1999).

44. "The Papacy is not other than the Ghost of the deceased Roman Empire, sitting crowned upon the grave thereof." Thomas Hobbes, *Leviathan,* Part IV at 47 (1651).

45. Gilmore, *supra* note 1, at 141.

46. *Id.* at 146.

47. Richard A. Posner, "Volume One of The Journal of Legal Studies—An Afterword," 1 *J. Legal Stud.* 437, 437 (1972). Compare, "Langdell's idea was that law is a science. He once explained how literally he took that doubtful proposition: '[A]ll the materials of that science [that is, law] are contained in printed books. . . . [T]he library is . . . to us all that the laboratories of the university are to the chemists and physicists, all that the museum of natural history is to the zoologists, all that the botanical garden is to the botanists. . . .'" G. Gilmore, *The Ages of Law* (1st ed., 1975) quoting an address by Langdell to the Harvard Law School Association in 1886, quoted in A. Sutherland, *The Law at Harvard,* at 175 (1967).

48. Gilmore, *supra* note 1, at 12–13.

49. *Id.* at 79–80.

50. *Id.* at 75.

51. See *id.* at 83 (noting that Llewellyn and Corbin's philosophies were at the "opposite pole" from Langdellianism).

52. Bruce Ackerman, 2 *We the People: Transformations* 3–31 (1998).

53. 410 U.S. 113 (1973).

54. 418 U.S. 683 (1974).

55. 520 U.S. 681 (1997).

56. 377 U.S. 533 (1964).

57. 469 U.S. 528 (1985).

58. 376 U.S. 254 (1964).

59. 531 U.S. 98 (2000).

60. Roberto Mangabeira Unger, "The Critical Legal Studies Movement," 96 *Harv. L. Rev.* 561, 570 (1983).

61. Carl von Clausewitz, *On War* 87 (ed. and trans. Michael Howard and Peter Paret, 1976 [1832]).

62. Pub. L. No. 88-352, 78 Stat. 241.

63. U.S.C. §§ 1973–1973bb-1 (2006).

64. See, e.g., Henry v. Clarksdale Mun. Separate Sch. Dist., 409 F.2d 682 (5th Cir. 1969); United States v. Greenwood Mun. Separate Sch. Dist., 406 F.2d 1086 (5th Cir. 1969); Graves v. Walton Cnty. Bd. of Educ., 403 F.2d 184 (5th Cir. 1968).

65. From which Unger later disassociated himself: "[I]t is a dead-end. It tempts the radical indeterminist into an intellectual and political desert, and abandons him there alone, disoriented, disarmed, and, at last, corrupted—by powerlessness." Roberto Unger, *What Should Legal Analysis Become?* 121 (1996).While Unger provided crucial theoretical underpinnings for CLS, it often seemed that his ideas about law were principally an expression of a more general position in law and social theory—see Jeremy Waldron, "Dirty Little Secret," Book Review of Roberto Unger's *What Should Legal Analysis Become?*, 98 *Col. L. Rev.* 510 (1998)—and this chapter makes no effort to address his rich thought in the intervening forty years since the publication of *Knowledge and Politics* (1976).

66. Roberto Unger, e-mail correspondence with the author, January 2, 2014.

67. Mark Tushnet, one of the most thoughtful members of the movement, had boldly written in 1981 that, were he a judge, he would determine "which result is, in the circumstances now exist-

ing, likely to advance the cause of socialism" and decide the case accordingly. "The Dilemmas of Liberal Constitutionalism," 42 *Ohio State Law Journal*, 421, 424 (1981).

68. Roberto Unger, *What Should Legal Analysis Become?*

69. But see Mark Tushnet, "Some Current Controversies in Critical Legal Studies," http://www.germanlawjournal.com/pdfs/Vol12-No1/PDF_Vol_12_No_01_290-299_Articles_Tushnet.pdf.

70. Duncan Kennedy, *The Rise and Fall of Classical Legal Thought*, xxxi (2006).

71. Henry James, *Hawthorne* 143 (1997).

72. Unger, e-mail correspondence with the author, January 2, 2014.

73. Ibid.

74. See Louis Menand, "What Is 'Critical Legal Studies'?: Radicalism for Yuppies," *The New Republic*, Mar. 17, 1986, at 20, 21 (noting that the purpose of CLS was to "expose the entire system of legal thought as an intellectual prison house").

75. Duncan Kennedy, "Legal Education and the Reproduction of Hierarchy," 32 *J. Legal Educ.* 591, 610 (1982).

76. Daniel Markovits, letter to the author, July 26, 2013.

77. Duncan Kennedy, "Rebels from Principle: Changing the Corporate Law Firm from Within," *Harv. Law School Bull.*, Fall 1981, at 39.

78. Mark V. Tushnet, "Dia-Tribe," 78 *Mich. L. Rev.* 694 (1980) (reviewing Lawrence H. Tribe, *American Constitutional Law* (1978)).

79. *Id.* at 615.

80. *Id.*

81. The Crits charged that they weren't alone in this tactic. The Yale Law School faculty was notable in its efforts to prevent the movement from gaining a foothold in New Haven, defending this posture by insisting on academic standards for appointment that seemed to their critics a false ground that was no more than a cover for the politics the Crits claimed always underlay such decisions. See Laura Kalman, *Yale Law School and the Sixties: Revolt and Reverberations* (2005).

82. See Mark G. Kelman, "Trashing," 36 *Stan. L. Rev.* 293 (1984).

83. *Cf.* Steven L. Winter, "The Next Century of Legal Thought?," 22 *Cardozo L. Rev.* 747, 748 (2001) (noting that CLS "reassert[ed] and reinvigorat[ed] . . . the claims that law is political and indeterminate").

84. Roberto Unger, *Knowledge and Politics* 295 (1975), though perhaps "Homo sibi Deus" would be a better motto for the CLS movement in general.

85. Arthur Allen Leff, "Memorandum," 29 *Stan. L. Rev.* 879, 879 (1977) (reviewing Roberto Mangabeira Unger, *Knowledge and Politics* (1975)).

86. See MacFarquhar, *supra* note 33, at 87 (noting that Law and Economics proponents claim that judges "in practice . . . had decided their cases as though they were trying to bring about the outcome that a free market would have produced.").

87. See Leff, *supra* note 23, at 458 (observing that the economic approach simply substitutes "human desire itself" for other values); see also Arthur Allen Leff, "Unspeakable Ethics, Unnatural Law," 1979 *Duke L.J.* 1229, 1229-30 ("[T]here cannot be any normative system ultimately based on anything except human will.").

88. Posner's view that "[the central] meaning of justice, perhaps the most common is—efficiency. . . . [because] in a world of scarce resources waste should be regarded as immoral," see Posner, *supra* note 40, at 30, begs a few questions: Is it obviously *wasteful* to give a kidney to a dying child even when, were it sold to the highest bidder, a kidney machine might then be purchased? Is it a waste to provide a superior education to an underprivileged student whose background makes it unlikely she will perform as well in the class as the prep school graduate whose place she took? Efficiency is a calculus of means; it does not supply ends.

89. See Louis Michael Seidman, "Critical Constitutionalism Now," 75 *Fordham L. Rev.* 575, 578-79 & n.14 (2006) (noting that critical legal theory evolved into structural, existential, and decisionist schools); see also Robert W. Gordon, "Critical Legal His-

tories," 36 *Stan. L. Rev.* 57, 98–102 & n.102 (1984) (noting critical legal theory's adoption of historiography); Thomas C. Heller,
"Structuralism and Critique," 36 *Stan. L. Rev.* 127, 129 (arguing
structuralism provides tools with which to explain particular critical legal theory arguments); J. M. Balkin, "Deconstructive Practice
and Legal Theory," 96 *Yale L.J.* 743, 23 n.60 (1987) (noting "decon-
struction of the philosophy of economic individualism is a favorite
topic of the Critical Legal Studies movement"); Jeffrey A. Standen,
Note, "Critical Legal Studies as an Anti-Positivist Phenomenon," 72
Va. L. Rev. 983, 992–94 (1986) (asserting critical legal theory movement aligns itself against positivism).

90. See Richard A. Posner, *How Judges Think* 9 (2008) ("[L]aw is
shot through with politics and with much else besides that does not
fit a legalist model of decision making.").

91. Grant Gilmore, "For Arthur Leff," 91 *Yale L.J.* 217 (1981).

92. *Id.* at 218.

93. See Charles L. Black, Jr., "Arthur Leff and His Law Dictionary," 94 *Yale L.J.* 1845 (1985). "Anecdotal evidence" is defined by
Leff as a "term of abuse in assessing a social science argument,"
Arthur A. Leff, "The Leff Dictionary of Law: A Fragment," 94 *Yale
L.J.* 1855, 2023 (1985); "approbate and reprobate" for accept and reject are Latinisms which Leff called "insufferably fancy," *id.* at 2046;
"abominable and detestable crime against nature" is a "rather enthusiastic euphemism . . . found in many nineteenth-century (and
some current) statutes, referring to a not fully specified range of
sexual crimes," *id.* at 1866.

94. R. P. Blackmur, "T. S. Eliot," in *Outsider at the Heart of Things*
38, 55 (1989).

95. Philip K. Howard, *The Collapse of the Common Good: How
America's Lawsuit Culture Undermines Our Freedom* 39 (2001).

96. Paul D. Carrington, "Of Law and the River," 34 *J. Legal Educ.*
222, 227 (1984).

97. In a fascinating observation, Daniel Markovits has noted
that the rise of the Law and Economics movement and its correla-
tive due process revolution are the result of the evolution of the

constitutional order of the industrial nation-state. "Once the state got into the business of providing as many goods to as many people as the modern state does, it needs an organizing method for sorting out what to do when for whom. That method must be at home in instrumental reason and it must work well with large amounts of data and many contingencies. Economics does this (I think someone once said that Utilitarianism was the first moral view at home in a probabilistic world).The method must also answer challenges to the legitimacy of countless decisions that simply would not have been taken in the past—due process does this. So in a way, the ideological disputes that have played out in law schools and in the bar are epiphenomenal. Given what the law was called on to regulate, the methods that have followed were nearly inevitable." See Markovits, *supra* note 76. Compare *id.* with Bobbitt, *supra* note 8, at 205–09.

98. Note the creation of the Office of Information and Regulatory Affairs, which was, until recently, headed by a champion of "judicial minimalism," the talented and prolific law professor Cass Sunstein.

99. 410 U.S. 113 (1973).

100. Washington v. Davis, 426 U.S. 229 (1976).

101. Adarand Constructors, Inc. v. Pena, 515 U.S. 200 (1995).

102. McAuliffe v. Mayor of New Bedford, 29 N.E. 517 (Mass. 1892). "There are few employments for hire in which the servant does not agree to suspend his constitutional right of free speech, as well as of idleness, by the implied terms of his contract. The servant cannot complain, as he takes the employment on the terms which are offered him." *Id.*

103. Tinker v. Des Moines Indep. Cmty. Sch. Dist., 393 U.S. 503, 511 (1969).

104. 558 U.S. 310, 372 (2010).

105. Goss v. Lopez, 419 U.S. 565, 574 (1975).

106. Wood v. Strickland, 420 U.S. 308, 322 (1975).

107. Cleveland Bd. of Educ. v. Loudermill, 470 U.S. 532, 542–46 (1985).

108. Adam J. White, "Ahead of His Class," *Wall St. J.* (Apr. 2, 2012), http://online.wsj.com/article/SB10001424052702304537904577279432126691786.html.

109. *Id.; cf.* WebMD, "Needless Medical Tests Costly," *CBS News* (May 9, 2006, 5:16 PM), http://www.cbsnews.com/news/needless-medical-tests-costly/ (discussing unnecessary medical tests generally).

110. See, e.g., Pearson v. Chung, Memorandum Opinion No. 08-758 (U.S. Dist. Ct. for the District of Columbia, July 23, 2009), in which an administrative law judge filed suit against the owner of a dry cleaner, demanding $67 million in damages as a result of the cleaner's failure to live up to a "satisfaction guaranteed" sign following the loss of the plaintiff's trousers.

111. Via the *Gideon* and *Miranda* cases that guaranteed an indigent defendant the right to a lawyer and to all defendants the right to remain silent without penalty. See Miranda v. Arizona, 384 U.S. 436 (1966); Gideon v. Wainwright, 372 U.S. 335 (1963).

112. Mapp v. Ohio, 367 U.S. 643, 655–56 (1961).

113. See Philip K. Howard, "History of American Law: Since 1968," in *The Oxford Companion to American Law* 392, 396 (Kermit L. Hall ed., 2002) at 392.

114. See Susan Ehrlich Martin and Nancy C. Jurik, *Doing Justice, Doing Gender: Women in Legal and Criminal Justice Occupations* 112 (2d ed. 2007) (noting number of lawyers in U.S. grew from 355,000 in 1971 to 806,000 in 1991).

115. 433 U.S. 350, 384 (1977). The opinion for the Court professes to be no more than an application of Virginia Pharmacy Board v. Virginia Citizens Consumer Council, 425 U.S. 748 (1976), which struck down a ban on commercial speech by licensed pharmacists. This suggested that by 1977, the unique status of lawyers as integral to the business of the state had far less salience than their role in their own business. Of course, as Holmes told us in *The Path of the Law,* practicing law is a business; the question is, what kind of business is it? "The danger is that the able and practical minded should look with indifference or distrust upon ideas

the connection of which with their business is remote. . . . [A]s Hegel says, 'It is in the end not the appetite, but the opinion, which has to be satisfied.'" Oliver Wendell Holmes, Jr., "The Path of the Law," 10 *Harv. L. Rev.* 457, 478 (1897). The damage to the opinion of lawyers as to themselves and of others does not seem to have concerned the Court. I should not be surprised to see, someday, vouchers replace public defenders.

116. Bates, 433 U.S. at 369–70.

117. 470 U.S. 274 (1985).

118. *Id.* at 275–76.

119. *Id.* at 283.

120. *Id.* at 283, 288. An earlier case, In re Griffiths, 413 U.S. 717, 729 (1973) had struck down the exclusion of aliens from a state's bar, and the Court apparently found this persuasive. But, as the dissent points out, Griffiths was an equal protection case, which has different standards than an Article IV privileges and immunities challenge. Piper, 470 U.S. at 298 n.4 (Rehnquist, J., dissenting). It may well be that a state has a higher burden when it attempts to exclude aliens as a class from a state office—for example, the governorship—than when the attempt to serve in a state-created office is made by a nonresident who brings his challenge on Article IV grounds. In either case, the important determination is not whether we consider lawyers officers of the court but whether we think their principal responsibility is to the state or the client.

121. Deborah L. Rhode, "The Professionalism Problem," 39 *Wm. & Mary L. Rev.* 283, 297 (1998).

122. Roger Scruton, "The Great Swindle," *Aeon* (Dec. 17, 2012).

123. See Menand, *supra* note 74, at 21 ("[T]he law is . . . the enforcer of a specific political ideology—the ideology of liberal capitalism."); *cf.* Richard Posner, "Why There Are Too Many Patents in America," *Atlantic*, July 12, 2012, http://www.theatlantic.com/business/archive/2012/07/why-there-are-too-many-patents-in-america/259725/ (describing the economic costs of the current patent system).

124. Presentation by Adam Liptak, Reporter, *N.Y. Times* (comparing his view with that of an earlier journalist covering the Su-

preme Court, Lyle Denniston) at conference, "Is America Governable?" University of Texas Law School, 26 January 2013.

125. "And quickly now the basketball scores, because we are running late: 110 to 102, 125 to 113, 131 to 127 and in an overtime duel, 95 to 94. Boy, that was a squeaker! Oh, and here's a partial score: Pittsburgh, 37." George Carlin, *Newscast 1967,* YouTube (uploaded Apr. 23, 2008), http://www.youtube.com/watch?v=yakmPBachUE.

126. Assaf Likhovski, "Two Horwitzian Journeys," in *Transformations in American Legal History: Essays in Honor of Professor Morton J. Horwitz* 300, 315–16 (Daniel W. Hamilton and Alfred L. Brophy eds., 2009) ("There is no way to discover why judges decide the way they do. Autonomous legal considerations; policy preferences; political ideology; jurisprudential notions; institutional constraints; strategic behavior; cultural biases; the influence of public opinion; the personality of judges, litigants, and lawyers; and countless other factors are all involved. Sorting them out and determining which of these factors influenced a specific decision or indeed a series of decisions is often an impossible task."). *Id.*

127. Cass. R. Sunstein et al., *Are Judges Political?: An Empirical Analysis of the Federal Judiciary* 82 (2006).

128. Adam Liptak, "Justices Agree to Agree, at Least for the Moment," *N.Y. Times* (May 27, 2013), http://www.nytimes.com/2013/05/28/us/supreme-court-issuing-more-unanimous-rulings.html.

129. See Society for the Advancement of American Philosophy, We-intentionality in Wilfrid Sellars' Systematic Moral Philosophy 7 (unpublished manuscript), available at www.american-philosophy.org/events/documents/2011_Program_files/S_miller_saap_2011_paper.doc ("To engage a question from the moral point of view is to attempt to engage a more-universal perspective—the perspective of one's community.").

130. Isaiah Berlin, "Two Concepts of Liberty," *in Four Essays on Liberty* (1969), http://www.wiso.uni-hamburg.de/fileadmin/wiso_vwl/johannes/Ankuendigungen/Berlin_twoconceptsofliberty.pdf.

131. See Philip Bobbitt, *Constitutional Interpretation* xvii, 184 (1991); *Cf.* Richard Rorty, *Contingency, Irony, and Solidarity* 46

(1989) (arguing civilized people recognize "the contingency of their own consciences" and yet "remain[] faithful to those consciences"). Critics of my use of the "conscience" as the tie-breaker when modalities conflict see this as a kind of cosmological constant, an added (and inelegant) fix for the problem posed by such conflicts. As the reader can see, I am unrepentant. If the medium is sometimes the message, the "problem" can sometimes be the solution.

132. See Grant Gilmore, *Stéphane Mallarmé: A Biography and an Interpretation,* PhD. Dissertation, Yale University, 1936.

133. See Philip Bobbitt, *The Garments of Court and Palace: Machiavelli and the World That He Made* at 104 (2013); and compare Philip Bobbitt, *Constitutional Fate: Theory of the Constitution* 248 (1982).

134. Jeremy Waldron, "Dirty Little Secret," 98 *Col. L. Rev.* 510 (1998).

135. A modality is the way in which we determine a statement to be true or false. We most often use this term with respect to possibility, impossibility, and necessity ('it is possible that p' or 'it is impossible that p' or 'it is necessarily the case that p' where 'p' is some proposition about the world). Thus it is possible that Gilmore was a law professor; it is impossible that I am Gilmore; it is necessarily the case that Gilmore was Gilmore. But there are many more modalities. Thus, among those formalized in modal logic, there are *temporal* modalities ('it was the case that p,' 'it has always been the case that p,' 'it will be the case that p') and *deontic* modalities ('it is obligatory that p,' 'it is permissible that p,' 'it is forbidden that p'); *epistemic* modalities ('it is known that p,' 'it cannot be determined that p,' 'it is not known that p') and *doxastic* modalities ('it is believed that p,' 'it is denied that p,' 'it is undecided that p').

In the constitutional law of the United States, there are six well-recognized modalities. For example, the modality of historical argument (sometimes called "originalism") determines a proposition purporting to construe a provision of the constitution to be true or false depending on whether the ratifiers of the text to be construed intended that it be construed in the manner proposed by the proposition, or did not so intend, or that it cannot be determined what their intentions as to this matter were.

One important point is that a modality is itself neither true nor false; it is the *way* in which propositions are determined to be true or false. The fact that the golden meter in Paris is stipulated to be one meter long does not mean that it is necessarily one meter long (the stipulation could have been otherwise), nor that it happens to be either longer or shorter than or exactly as long as one meter long, because the only way in which this can be determined is by reference to the stipulation, not by measurement. The modalities of constitutional argument could be different; the fact that they are what they are allows us to go on, allows us to determine the truths of any constitutional proposition except the one referring to the truths of the modalities themselves.

Suppose we were to treat a modality as a proposition. For example, consider this proposition: "In determining the meaning of a constitutional provision, judges should be guided by the intentions of the ratifiers of the provision to be construed." Now suppose that a conscientious application of historical argument to the problem yields the rule: "The ratifiers did not intend that their intentions should guide judges in the interpretation of a constitutional provision." Applying that rule to determine the truth or falsity of the proposition, one would have to conclude that the proposition was false. But if it was false, the rule applied must also be false; and if the rule applied—the modality—is false, then the proposition is true. In fact, neither truth nor falsity affects the status of the modality, which is sanctified by practice, and thus it is *practice* that legitimates, not truth or falsity according to a metric external to the practice.

136. Jack Balkin, "Preface to Constitutional Interpretation," unpublished manuscript on file with the *Yale Law Journal.*

137. *Id.*

138. A small sample includes Akhil Reed Amar, "Intratextualism," 112 *Harv. L. Rev.* 747, 789 (1999) (arguing that intratextual argument is not an appeal to original meaning and is "distinct

from standard forms of argument based on history and original intent"); Jamal Greene, "On the Origins of Originalism," 88 *Tex. L. Rev.* 1, 64, 82–88 (2009); Robert Post, "Theories of Constitutional Interpretation," 30 *Representations* 13 (1990); Richard Primus, "The Functions of Ethical Originalism," 88 *Tex. L. Rev.* 79 (2009); Jack M. Balkin, "The New Originalism and the Uses of History," *Fordham Law Review,* Forthcoming, Yale Law School, Public Law Working Paper No. 303; Keith E. Whittington, *Constitutional Interpretation: Textual Meaning, Original Intent, and Judicial Review* (2001); Richard H. Fallon, Jr., "A Constructivist Coherence Theory of Constitutional Interpretation," 100 *Harv. L. Rev.* 1189, 1244, 1254 (1987); Philip Bobbitt, *Constitutional Fate: Theory of the Constitution* (1982); see also Philip Bobbitt, *Constitutional Interpretation* (1991).

139. For example, in 2008 the *Harvard Law Review* published a lengthy, two-part article arguing that the virtually universal assumption that Congress may not regulate the president's tactical oversight of wartime operations is founded on an egregious oversight. "The notion, supposedly deeply embedded in the Constitutional plan, that the Commander-in-Chief Clause prevents the Congress from interfering with the President's operational discretion in wartime by 'directing the conduct of campaigns'" is belied by a careful review of the actual practices of the president and Congress from the founding up to 1950. Thus, despite its unreflective reaffirmation in the recent *Hamdan* case, "the argument for a substantive preclusive power must proceed, if at all, by defending a reversal of our [historic practices]." David J. Barron and Martin S. Ledermann, "The Commander-in-Chief at the Lowest Ebb—Framing the Problem, Doctrine and Original Understanding," 121 *Harv. L. Rev.* 689, 696 (2008).

The authors indeed made a valuable discovery. But was theirs a constitutional argument? If it is true that, until relatively recently, our practice—which is to say our *doctrinal* understanding—was otherwise than it has recently been, this does not count against more recent doctrine. Doctrine provides for its own overruling; modification is allowed.

The authors pose this choice to the Executive branch: presidents "can build upon a practice rooted in a fundamental acceptance of a legitimacy of congressional control over the conduct of campaigns that prevailed without substantial challenge through World War II. Or they can cast their lot with the more recent view, espoused by to some extent by most—but not all—modern Presidents, that the principle of exclusive control over the conduct of war provides the baseline for which to begin thinking about the Commander-in-Chief's proper place in the constitutional structure."

To see how ambitious this argument is, imagine its authors had written: Courts can build upon a practice—segregation—rooted in the fundamental acceptance of the state's role in federalism that prevailed without substantial challenge into the late 1950s; or they can cast their lot with the more recent view that racial discrimination is unconstitutional. Common understandings about the intentions of the ratifiers can be overturned by better research, more careful inferences, etc. But doctrinal argument—that is, the record of congressional and presidential practice that parallels the decision of cases and controversies by courts—is dispositive only to the extent of the most recent "holdings." If earlier presidents did in fact act as the article's authors claimed, this is of far less significance than how Congress and the President acted in 1949 and, of course, more recently.

140. For a moving example, see Frederick Douglass's use of textual argument to show that the pre–Civil War constitution did not tolerate, much less endorse, slavery, Philip Bobbitt, "The Constitutional Canon," in *Legal Canons* 400 (Sanford Levinson and J. M. Balkin eds., 2000).

141. See Andre LeDuc, "The Relationship of Constitutional Law to Philosophy: Five Lessons from the Originalism Debate," 12 *Geo. J.L. Pub. Pol'y* 99 (2014).

142. For a brief sample, see Jack M. Balkin and Sanford Levinson, "The Processes of Constitutional Change: From Partisan Entrenchment to the National Surveillance State," 75 *Fordham L. Rev.* 489 (2006); Jack Goldsmith, *The Terror Presidency: Law and Judgment Inside the Bush Administration* 96 (2007); Trevor W. Morrison, "Constitutional Avoidance in the Executive Branch," 106 *Colum.*

L. Rev. 1189 (2006); H. Jefferson Powell, *The President's Authority over Foreign Affairs* (2002); Kim Lane Scheppele, "We Are All Post-9/11 Now," 75 *Fordham L. Rev.* 607 (2006); Bruce Ackerman, *Before the Next Attack: Preserving Civil Liberties in an Age of Terrorism* (2006); David J. Barron and Martin S. Lederman, "The Commander in Chief at the Lowest Ebb—Framing the Problem, Doctrine, and Original Understanding," 121 *Harv. L. Rev* 689 (2008); David Barron and Martin S. Lederman, "The Commander-in-Chief at the Lowest Ebb—A Constitutional History," 121 *Harv. L. Rev* 941 (2008); Robert Chesney and Jack Goldsmith, "Terrorism and the Convergence of Criminal and Military Detention Models," 60 *Stan. L. Rev.* 1079, 1080 n.2 (2008). Matthew Waxman, "National Security Federalism in the Age of Terror," 64 *Stanford L. Rev.* 289 (2012); David Pozen, "The Leaky Leviathan: Why Government Condemns and Condones Unlawful Disclosures of Information," 127 *Harv. L. Rev.* 512 (2013).

143. See Philip Bobbitt, *The Shield of Achilles: War, Peace, and the Course of History* (2002), which argued that the epochal wars that consolidated and transformed the constitutional order of individual states since the Renaissance ratified each triumphant constitutional order by means of a constitution for the society of states, negotiated and consented to at the great peace congresses that ended these wars.

144. Barnes v. Glen Theatre, Inc., 501 U.S. 560, 563 (1992). Note also the recent play *Arguendo,* in which the theatrical troupe Elevator Repair Service stages an artfully assembled theatrical collage of the opinion, complete with a group of exotic dancers. See Ben Brantley, "Full-Frontal Justice, a Matter of Redress," *N.Y. Times,* Sept. 24, 2013, http://www.nytimes.com/2013/09/25/theater/reviews/arguendo-by -elevator-repair-service-at-the-public-theater.html—a performance of which at the New York Public Theater the present author, implausibly, introduced.

145. See The Federalist Nos. 2–5 (John Jay).

146. Jonathan Macey, "Law and the Social Sciences," Yale Law School Faculty Scholarship Series, Paper 1451, at 173 (1997). Not every scholar was so smitten with the prospect of transcending mere personal values; see Anthony Kronman, *The Lost Lawyer: Failing Ideals of the Legal Profession* (1993).

147. Reader's Report, undated, Yale University Press, on file with the *Yale Law Journal.*

148. Adam Liptak, "The Lackluster Reviews That Lawyers Love to Hate," *N.Y. Times,* Oct. 21, 2013, citing Thomas A. Smith, "The Web of Law," San Diego Legal Studies Research Paper No. 06-11 (Spring 2005).

149. Randall Jarrell, *Poetry and Age* (1953) at 72–73.

150. "Radical feminists may argue that treating women as bearers and mothers of children merely perpetuates the subjugation of women by men, but of what value is this argument to you as an advocate confronting an audience that does not agree? You can develop a similar criticism of family law using economics. Take, for example, Lloyd Cohen's article in the *Journal of Legal Studies,* using an economic approach to reach a result perfectly consistent with feminist perspectives on marriage and on the exploitation of women in the marital context. [Cohen shows] that the present value of a wife's human capital contribution to a marriage declines faster and earlier than that of a husband's, arguing that this disparate rate of decline induces the husband to seek divorce, and examining various possible legal innovations that might ameliorate this result." See Macey, *ibid.* It is hard to think that there are many persons who would cavil at the first approach but swallow the "economic approach" instead, especially when, as the author notes, its purpose is to achieve results consistent with the objectives and values of "radical feminists." Nor would I like to be the husband who points out these statistical results to his wife, whatever her views on feminism.

151. S. Ct. 2612 (2013).

152. *Id.* at 2620.

153. *Id.* at 2618.

154. *Id.* at 2631.

155. See Grant Gilmore, "Legal Realism: Its Cause and Cure," 70 *Yale L.J.* 1037, 1043 (1961) (arguing that a court, when faced with a "gap in the statutory scheme," should reason "according to the basic principles of the common law").

156. See Guido Calabresi, *A Common Law for the Age of Statutes* 1–2 (1982) (offering common law approach as a response to the proliferation of statutes).

157. It is easy to misconstrue this point—that the American nation-state burst on the world scene with Sherman's military tactics of total war that attacked the *nation* directly rather than limiting itself to its armed forces, and with Lincoln's immortal Emancipation Proclamation that aimed to reorder the outcome of the market to achieve greater equality. It's not that the Emancipation Proclamation was an act *against* the market; far from it. Emancipation vastly expanded markets; where once there had been four million slaves, unable to make contracts, there were now four million new buyers and sellers, employers and employees. See Reader's Report, October 3, 2013, Yale University Press, on file with the *Yale Law Journal*. Industrial nation-states aren't hostile to the growth of markets, they simply see themselves as the means by which markets should be governed, avoiding the most catastrophic outcomes and encouraging economic activity that is beneficial to those political values as to which the market, unaided and ungoverned by the state, is indifferent.

158. See the discussions of the transition from late nineteenth- and twentieth-century industrial nation-state to twenty-first-century informational market state in Philip Bobbitt, *The Garments of Court and Palace: Machiavelli and the World That He Made*, at 172–76 (2013); Bobbitt, *supra* note 35, at 205–13; Philip Bobbitt, *Terror and Consent: The Wars for the Twenty-First Century* 85–90 (2008).

159. Daniel Kahneman and Amos Tversky, "Prospect Theory: An Analysis of Decision under Risk," 47 *Econometrica* 263–91 (1979).

160. Christine Jolls, Cass R. Sunstein, and Richard Thaler, "A Behavioral Approach to Law and Economics," Yale Law School Faculty Scholarship Series, Paper 1765, http://digitalcommons.law .yale.edu/fss_papers/1765.

161. Ian Ayres, *Carrots and Sticks: Unlock the Power of Incentives to Get Things Done* (2010); Cass R. Sunstein, "Nudges.gov: Behavioral Economics and Regulation" (February 16, 2013), Forthcoming, in *Oxford Handbook of Behavioral Economics and the Law* (Eyal Zamir

and Doron Teichman eds.). Available at SSRN: http://ssrn.com/abstract=2220022 or http://dx.doi.org/10.2139/ssrn.2220022.

162. McDonald v. Chicago, 130 S. Ct. 3020 (2010); District of Columbia v. Heller, 554 U.S. 570 (2008).

163. See *Constitutional Interpretation,* at 167 (Friendly exchange with Hand).

164. *Cf.* T. S. Eliot, "East Coker," *The Four Quartets* (1940); see also "Editors' Introduction," 84 *Yale L.J.* 1022, 1027 (1975): "Sometime ago, speaking of the law itself, [Gilmore] had written, 'The more things change, the French proverb reminds us, the more they are the same: our gains, it may be, are illusory, but so are our losses.'"

165. "East Coker," *supra.*

166. Ecclesiastes 3:22, The Holy Bible, King James Version.

Index

abolition, ix, 33
Abraham Lincoln bar, 20
academia. *See* law schools
Ackerman, Bruce, x, 114
activism, judicial. *See* courts
admiralty law, 27, 185*n*54, 186*n*58, 187*nn*58–59; federalization of (pre–Civil War period), 27
Age of Anxiety, 61–88, 105
Age of Consent, 100–149
Age of Discovery, 17–36, 114, 136
Age of Faith, 37–60, 92, 105, 114
agriculture, 22, 33, 110, 194*n*33
Allegheny College case, 177*n*18
American Bar Association, 62; codification of commercial law after *1900,* 62–63
American Indians, 8, 165*n*32
American law, xiii–xvi; Age of Anxiety, 61–88, 105; Age of Consent, 100–149; Age of Discovery, 17–36, 114, 136; Age of Faith, 37–60, 92, 105, 114; analysis of judicial behavior, 131–35; apparent death of federal law principle (*Erie R.R. v. Tompkins*), 84; beginnings of, 7–10; changing orientation between economics and, 144–47; courts in post–Civil War period, 54–57; Critical Legal Studies, 115–24; establishment of national reporter system,

53–54; future of, 147–49; greater focus on the individual, 125–28; hostility to England, 20; influence of frontier spirit on, 19–20; influence of Lord Mansfield on development of, 21–22; judicial power (pre–Civil War period), 31–32; Langdellian literature, 51–54; Law and Economics movement, 107–15; legitimacy of constitutional law questioned, 102–5; modal approach, 135–37, 204*n*135, 205*n*135, 206*n*139, 207*n*139; national uniformity and, 22–26, 29, 31, 37, 144, 146; periods of, 11–12; plummeting public perception of lawyers, 128–31; pre–Civil War codification movement, 23–31; pre–Civil War literature, 20–21, 25–27; professionalization after *1820,* 20–21; rebirth of federal law principle in post-*Erie* period, 84–85; relationship to English law, 9–10, 17–21, 58; rights revolution, 125–28; roles of state and federal law under the federal constitution, 18–19, 22; Roman law and pre–Civil War law compared, 35–36; second-generation Legal Realism, 101–7; slavery and, 32–35; Story on, 25–31;